RECIPES FROM

Wine Country

RECIPES FROM
Wine Country

TONY DE LUCA

whitecap

LIBRARY AND ARCHIVES CANADA CATALOGUING IN PUBLICATION

De Luca, Tony
    Recipes from wine country / Tony de Luca.

Includes index.
ISBN 1-55285-605-4

    1. Cookery (Wine) I. Title.

TX726.D44 2004   641.6'22   C2004-904589-X

Printed and bound in Canada
Second printing, 2005

IMPORTANT Some of the recipes in this book call for the use of raw eggs. Pregnant women, the elderly, young children and anyone with a compromised immune system are advised against the consumption of raw eggs. You may wish to consider the use of pasteurized eggs. <www.aeb.org/safety> provides updated information on eggs and food safety.

PROOFREAD BY Lesley Cameron

COVER AND INTERIOR DESIGN Stacey Noyes

COVER AND FOOD PHOTOGRAPHY Joseph Chan 陳樹恩 and Steven Chan 陳樹勳 / ARTiculation Group, Toronto

COVER AND FOOD PHOTOGRAPHY ART DIRECTION Ivy Wong 黃雅慧 and Joseph Chan 陳樹恩

FOOD STYLING Tony de Luca

ELECTRONIC PHOTO CORRECTION Debbie Chan / ARTiculation Group, Toronto

ADDITIONAL ACCENT PHOTOGRAPHY Tony de Luca, David Martin, Joseph Chan, Steven Chan and Hillebrand Estates Winery

contents

6

acknowledgements

Early in the process of putting together this cookbook, I was asked why I wanted to pursue this project. There are two answers.

First, this book has helped me to satisfy a constant need to define myself through my profession and my craft, and to provide a nurturing service to strangers so that I can repay a significant debt. It's a debt of gratitude for my life.

As a baby, I would not eat. I was malnourished and when all hope for my survival was gone, a priest was called and I was given the last rites. Luckily for me my godmother wouldn't give up and she saved my life by feeding me. So, for me, generosity with food is not an option. I acknowledge my godmother with thanks.

Secondly, I wanted to do it for my two sons, Matthew and Nicholas. I wanted to put all of my experiences, my culinary vision and my accomplishments in one form that they could see when they grow up, to help them understand why I wasn't always at home with them. I want my sons to see this book one day and appreciate that my time working away from them was not wasted. I want them to devote their lives to their passions and the true happiness that will follow. To my sons, thank you.

One does not fulfill a lifelong dream without help, and I have a big group of supporters to thank:

My wife, Kaleen: for her unwavering support, encouragement, advice and love that all help me to be a good father and chef.

Mom and Dad: for the sacrifices they made for us kids. Their example has taught me that hard work, passion and dedication are the foundation of all that is good in life.

Greg Berti and Bob Davis: for believing in me and hiring me at Hillebrand back in 1996. After all this time I still believe I have the best chef job in Canada and not a day goes by that I am not grateful for being here.

Mark Torrance and Sherri Lockwood: for their initiative, counsel, guidance and belief in the book project.

My brother, Danny de Luca, and my sister-in-law, Gacia de Luca: for all their support over the years.

I want to thank all the people I have cooked with over the years, particularly the opening team at Langdon Hall: Chef Nigel Didcock, a true friend and gifted cuisinier, Paul Boehmer, Jerome Chenet, Todd Clarmo, Alan Kehl and Jason Parsons, and owners Bill Bennett and Mary Beaton.

Robert Buchanan and Sue Baby: for their friendship and sense of humor. Robert told me about the opportunity

at Hillebrand in the first place, so special thanks to him.

Reinhardt Sherrer-Henning: for his loyalty and inspiration during our years at the Millcroft and the Doctor's House.

The Hillebrand kitchen and restaurant team that worked with me during the writing of this book, especially Ross Midgley, the archetypal sous chef and one of the finest chefs I have ever met.

Laura Buder: for being such a great help in the writing of this book. Laura worked hard on this project as a recipe tester/fixer and her influence is much appreciated.

Michael Bonacini: for being a role model chef for me at the beginning of my career.

I especially want to thank Geoffrey Bray Cotton, my friend and confidante, for believing in me, helping me with words of counsel, encouragement, laughter, helping me to find great staff and even doing the washing up(!!). You are a tremendous person and thank you for your friendship.

Nicolette Novak: special thanks to her for the use of The Good Earth Cooking School, where many of these photos were taken.

Robert McCullough, Alison Maclean and the gang at

Whitecap Books: thanks to everyone for making my job so much easier when I was working on the book. It has been a pleasure to meet and work with all of you.

Joseph Chan and his talented team, his brother, Steven, and his wife, Ivy: for all their creative energy and for the photographs that perfectly capture my recipes. They made the food photography fun and their work is above and beyond my highest hopes for the photos.

Last but certainly not least, I would like to thank my friends. True friendship in this business is sometimes difficult to establish, so the friends I have I cherish greatly. My heartfelt thanks to all of you who have entered my life and made it so fulfilling.

preface

I remember first hearing Tony's name from a young apprentice who had been hired at Hillebrand's new restaurant. I was intrigued by what I heard about the talented new chef.

Well, that was several years ago now. Since then, Tony and I have shared many wonderful meals together at tables both grand and simple. Our friendship is peppered with memories of marvelous foods and flavors, garnished with a healthy dollop of laughter.

Over the years, I have come to understand the philosophy behind Tony's approach to cooking. It's grounded and humble, anchored by his integrity. He celebrates the gifts of Mother Nature's bounty, letting the pure flavors sing. He honors our producers, stewards of this great land, seeking out the best from across Canada. He encourages the bright young chefs who labor at his side, nurturing their talents, admonishing them to always remember a simple message: it's a privilege to be a cook and to provide the most fundamental of our human needs. This is a message that is too often lost in the current era of celebrity chefs.

There is nothing superficial about Tony or his cooking. What you see is what you get. His motivating force is an unabashed passion for living. His pleasures are simple and many. Inevitably, that passion involves a lovingly prepared meal, a good bottle of wine, a table of friends, family and laughter.

This book is a tribute to food as it is meant to be — simple and true, created with passion, integrity and love. This is Tony's legacy to Niagara wine country cooking. Enjoy!

Nicolette Novak

introduction

There are few experiences in life that are as complete, pleasurable and rewarding as sitting down to a meal with family and friends. And when the flavors of the food and wine are in harmony we experience something beyond our expectations; meals can bring us joy.

The goal of this cookbook is to encourage joy in everyday dining through simple preparations and a "wine centric" approach to the meal planning. Once you have chosen a wine for your meal, you may then choose from a variety of recipes organized by wine and season. You may choose simple recipes, or ones that are more challenging, to execute your own perfect marriage of food and wine.

As Chef of Hillebrand Estates Winery Restaurant, I have tried to create a unique style of cuisine using wine as the framework to present the bountiful Niagara produce. I've had the opportunity to explore the riches of our region over the past several years. In that time, I have nurtured a close relationship with a variety of local artisanal growers. From fresh figs and heirloom vegetables to free range chicken and beef, the growers make our wine country cuisine possible.

At the restaurant, our culinary emphasis is on the seasonal ingredients of our region. With such an abundance of quality products, the recipes almost write themselves: sweet peas with baby beets in June, apricots with chanterelles and Riesling in July, peaches with basil and corn in August, fava beans with pearl potatoes in September. Our cuisine respects this bounty, emphasizing the ripe goodness and freshness of each ingredient. We care for each item, admiring and enjoying its integrity. We gently coax out the flavors with the latest culinary techniques. Our food is never contrived. We simply follow the subtle direction of our own "gout de terroir."

I strongly believe that food and wine is as natural a relationship as can be found. In the restaurant, highlighting the affinity of food and wine is our primary mandate. Having the good fortune to work side by side with a winemaker and a forager affords me a closer understanding of the intrinsic way food and wine work together. This book is an exploration of that relationship. I have organized the recipes by grape varieties to make it easier for the home cook to pair food and wine. My hope is that you will use this book throughout the year to discover your own unique and personal wine country cuisine.

Spring

Spiced Salmon
Marinated in Molasses

Canadian Crab Fritters

Scallops
Marinated in Sparkling Wine

Spice-Scented Lobster
with Anchovy Broth

Terrine of Smoked Salmon,
Spinach and Anchovy Butter

Summer

Fillet of Salmon
Baked in Parchment
with Sparkling Wine

Rainbow Trout
with Sparkling Wine,
Grape and Cream Sauce

Pickerel in Saffron
and Sparkling Wine Broth

Lemon Grass Shrimp Skewers

Sparkling

CHAMPAGNE, SPUMANTE, CAVE AND SEKT ARE ALL NAMES for sparkling wine. Champagne, the most famous sparkling wine of all, is made in a specific area of France: Champagne.

Out of respect for the appellation, wine made outside this geographic area is called not Champagne but sparkling wine. In North America, we use the term sparkling wine as a generic name for all wines that contain bubbles.

There are many varieties and styles of this wine, so it is useful to know what you're looking for. First of all, the sweetness factor: a wine described as "dry" or "demi-sec" is actually quite sweet. A wine labeled "sec" is also sweet, which is strange because that is the French word for dry. For dry and bone dry, look for wines labeled "brut" or "brut nature."

There are very few beverages I can think of that carry the aura of sparkling wine and Champagne. From the serious occasions in our lives to the frivolous and jovial, from sombre events to sporting event celebrations, it is always appropriate to pop the cork on a fresh bottle. Do you recall ever refusing a glass of sparkling wine when it was offered? Do your guests shun you because you serve it before a meal? I didn't think so!! And if you think about it, is the world not more friendly and tolerant, when seen through the tiny bubbles rushing to the surface of your glass?

Sparkling wines are usually blends of three varietals: Pinot Noir, Pinot Meunier and Chardonnay.

My first memory of drinking Champagne was during

Autumn

Duck Prosciutto Salad
   with Celery Root Remoulade

Lentil Soup with Duck Confit

Aged Cheddar and Rosemary Soufflé

Wine Country Duck Burger

Winter

Windsor Arms Creamy Liver Pâté

Harvest Squash Soup
   with Buttermilk and Oysters

Foie Gras with Icewine, Almond
   and Dried Apricot Sauté

Scallops with Crab on Basil Brut Syrup

Vanilla-Cured Arctic Char
   with Winter Greens and Risotto

Wine

my apprenticeship at the Windsor Arms Hotel in Toronto. My friend and co-apprentice, Daryl Grant, and I saved our money for weeks so we could go out to dinner in a very posh new restaurant in the Beaches. When we got there and were presented with the huge wine list, we decided to drink the only wine we could recognize by name. We ordered Champagne (actually 4 different bottles) and enjoyed it for the complete 6-course experience. Back then, I wasn't so much interested in knowing the complexities of food and wine pairing, but I do remember being impressed by the intensity of each flavor. At the time I attributed this to the skill of the chef, but now I realize that it was more likely the effect of the Champagne. The lesson of that evening was that sparkling wine has the ability to partner with a remarkable range of foods. It has an affinity for almost all food, especially salty, spicy and rich foods.

The effect of drinking sparkling wine when eating is that the wine refreshes, cleans and reinvigorates your palate, causing your mouth to taste the food as if it were your first bite, every time. I believe that you could drink only Champagne during a meal and still be completely satisfied.

This chapter offers a seasonal selection of foods, both appetizers and larger meals, that can be enjoyed in the company of sparkling wine. As a chef, I have come to regard this wine not only as a great drinking wine but also (as you will notice in the recipes) as an integral ingredient in my wine country cuisine.

Ingredients for the salmon

1 cup • 250 mL		**sea salt**
½ cup • 125 mL		**granulated sugar**
2 lbs. • 1 kg		**fresh salmon, pin bones removed and scaled**
1 cup • 250 mL		**coriander, finely chopped**
1 cup • 250 mL		**fresh parsley, finely chopped**
½ cup • 125 mL		**shallots, finely chopped**

Spiced Salmon Marinated in Molasses

This is a unique twist on traditional gravlax. Thinly sliced and served with warm dill scones, it makes a memorable hors d'oeuvre, or even an elegant starter to a fancy dinner. Rumor has it that I have used this deliciously moist and tasty salmon in my lunchtime sandwich on occasion. I can neither confirm nor deny this.

Combine the salt and sugar. Sprinkle half of the salt/sugar mix on a cookie sheet. Lay the salmon on top of the salt/sugar mix, skin-side down. Coat the top of the salmon with the remaining mix. Combine the coriander, parsley and shallots in a food processor and process until smooth. Pour this over the salmon. Cover with plastic wrap and refrigerate for 36 hours.

Remove from the refrigerator and wash off the salt cure and seasonings under cool running water. Using a kitchen towel, pat the salmon dry. Reserve.

MAKES 10–12 APPETIZER SERVINGS
OR 30 HORS D'OEUVRES SERVINGS.
(Unused salmon can be kept refrigerated for up to 2 weeks if tightly wrapped, or frozen for up to 1 month.)

Ingredients

1 cup • 250 mL		**molasses**
1 Tbsp. • 15 mL		**cayenne pepper**
1 Tbsp. • 15 mL		**ground coriander**
5		**bay leaves**

for the marinade

In a small saucepot set over medium-low heat combine all the ingredients and bring to a gentle boil. Reduce heat to a simmer and cook for 5 minutes, stirring frequently to prevent burning. Remove from the heat and let cool. Pour the molasses marinade over the cured salmon. Return to the refrigerator and marinate overnight. Slice the salmon into thin strips and serve.

Ingredients

pinch		**kosher salt**
pinch		**granulated sugar**
1½ cups	375 mL	**all-purpose flour, sifted**
¾ cup	175 ml	**sparkling wine**
2		**eggs, separated**
1 lb.	500 g	**Dungeness or other Canadian crabmeat**
4 cups	1 L	**oil for deep frying**
pinch		**cayenne pepper**

Canadian Crab Fritters

Crab is one of Canada's great seafood treasures. There are many crabs on the market and spring is the ideal time to eat them. Dungeness crab may look intimidating, but it is a supremely tasty meat. A rich, yeasty sparkling wine will match perfectly with the delicate taste of the crab fritters.

Place the salt, sugar and flour in a small bowl and make a well. Pour the sparkling wine and the egg yolks into the middle of the well and whisk slowly to combine. Cover with plastic wrap, store somewhere warm for 30 minutes then fold in the crabmeat.

Whip the egg whites to stiff peaks and fold into the batter. Half-fill a deep saucepan with peanut oil and heat to 350°F (180°C). Spoon dollops of the crab mixture into the oil and fry for 2 to 3 minutes. When the fritters are golden brown, transfer them to a tray lined with kitchen towel to absorb excessive grease.

Serve immediately.

MAKES 12 FRITTERS

Mustard Chervil Mayonnaise

Ingredients

2		**egg yolks**
1 Tbsp.	15 mL	**Dijon mustard**
2 Tbsp.	30 mL	**sherry wine vinegar**
1 cup	250 mL	**olive oil**
3		**shallots, finely minced**
2 Tbsp.	30 mL	**chervil, finely minced**
		kosher salt and white pepper to taste

In a small mixing bowl whisk the egg yolks, mustard and vinegar. Slowly add the oil to emulsify. Add the shallots and chervil. Season with salt and pepper. Serve with crab fritters.

Scallops
Marinated in Sparkling Wine

Sparkling wine is wonderful to drink. The tiny bubbles add sophistication and a sense of celebration to any event. It is also a great ingredient in wine country cooking. Those happy little bubbles of CO_2 work magic to transform sea scallops into the most delicate shellfish you will ever taste. This is my version of the famous Mexican seviche.

Ingredients

¹⁄₄ cup	•	50 mL	**lime juice**
¹⁄₄ cup	•	50 mL	**olive oil**
¹⁄₂ cup	•	125 mL	**sparkling wine**
1 Tbsp.	•	15 mL	**coriander, finely chopped**
1 tsp.	•	5 mL	**lightly toasted mustard seeds**
2 tsp.	•	10 mL	**fresh ginger, finely grated**
1 tsp.	•	5 mL	**granulated sugar**
pinch			**cayenne pepper**
1 lb.	•	500 g	**fresh sea scallops**

Add all the ingredients except the scallops to a large bowl and whisk to combine. Add the scallops and cover the bowl with plastic wrap. Refrigerate for 3 hours. Remove the scallops from the marinade. Discard the marinade and serve the scallops.

MAKES 6 SERVINGS

Spice-Scented Lobster
with Anchovy Broth

Many people believe that the best way to enjoy lobster is steamed with drawn butter and a sprinkle of sea salt. I would never argue with personal taste preferences, but lobster is incredibly versatile and can be enjoyed with many flavors without losing its tasty integrity. This recipe uses the whole lobster, from shell to meat. Do not eliminate the anchovies—they are the backbone of the recipe.

Ingredients

1		bay leaf
1 Tbsp. • 15 mL		coriander seeds
2 tsp. • 10 mL		mustard seeds
2 tsp. • 10 mL		mace
1		clove
1/2		cinnamon stick
1/2		vanilla pod, chopped
6		lobsters, pre-cooked (page 109)
1/4 cup • 50 mL		olive oil
1		onion, chopped
1		leek, chopped
1		carrot, peeled and chopped
2		tomatoes, chopped
1/2 cup • 125 mL		white wine
1/2 cup • 125 mL		brandy

Combine the bay leaf, coriander seeds, mustard seeds, mace, clove, cinnamon and vanilla in a small sauté pan. Toast over medium heat, stirring frequently, until the spices have become fragrant, about 5 minutes. Reserve.

Remove the lobster meat from the shells and reserve both. Reserve 6 tails and claws.

In a large soup pot, heat the olive oil to medium high and add the onion, leek and carrot. Sauté until the vegetables have softened, about 10 minutes, and add the reserved spices.

Add the tomatoes, wine, brandy and lobster shells. Pour in enough cold water to cover the shells and bring to a simmer. Continue to simmer for $1^1/_2$ hours, skimming away any foam that rises to the surface. Strain the liquid through a sieve and discard the solids. Return the liquid to the pot and reduce until only 2 cups/500 mL of liquid remain. Reserve this stock.

MAKES 6 SERVINGS
recipe continued on next page

Ingredients

2 Tbsp.	· 30 mL	**unsalted butter**
2		**shallots, finely diced**
$\frac{1}{2}$ cup	· 125 mL	**carrot, peeled and julienned**
$\frac{1}{2}$ cup	· 125 mL	**celery, peeled and julienned**
$\frac{1}{2}$ cup	· 125 mL	**shiitake mushrooms, julienned**
1 Tbsp.	· 15 mL	**anchovy fillet, finely chopped**
2		**tomatoes, seeded and julienned**
2 cups	· 500 mL	**Spice-Scented Lobster Stock (page 17)**
$\frac{1}{2}$ cup	· 125 mL	**sparkling wine**
1		**lemon, zest and juice of**
6		**reserved lobster tails and claws**
1 Tbsp.	· 15 mL	**coriander, chopped**

Anchovy Broth

Heat a medium-sized saucepot over medium heat and add the butter. When the butter has completely melted add the shallots, carrot, celery, mushrooms, anchovy and tomatoes. Cook, stirring frequently, for about 10 minutes or until the vegetables start to soften.

When the vegetables have wilted slightly add the lobster stock, wine and lemon zest and juice. Bring to a gentle simmer and reduce the liquid to about 2 cups (500 mL).

Add the reserved lobster meat and turn off the heat. Add the coriander. Divide the lobster meat and anchovy vegetable broth among 6 bowls.

Ingredients

2 cups	· 500 mL	**unsalted butter, softened**
3		**anchovy fillets, finely chopped**
2		**lemons, zest of, blanched and finely chopped**
1 tsp.	· 5 mL	**cayenne pepper**
2 lbs.	· 1 kg	**smoked salmon, sliced**
½ cup	· 125 mL	**chives, finely chopped**
2		**large bunches fresh spinach leaves, blanched and patted dry**

Terrine of Smoked Salmon, Spinach
and Anchovy Butter

The late Jean-Louis Palladin was a remarkable chef. I worked for him at the Watergate Hotel in Washington DC in 1989 and I can still recall vividly many intense and defining culinary experiences in his kitchen. He was a highly energetic, demanding, intense and creative chef.

In a food processor, combine the butter, anchovies and lemon zest. Process for 1 minute, to combine. Sprinkle in the cayenne pepper and combine well.

Transfer the anchovy butter to a small bowl. Using a pastry brush "paint" the anchovy butter on the inside surface a terrine mold. Line the mold with sliced smoked salmon.

Fill the mold with alternating layers of anchovy butter, spinach and smoked salmon, finishing with smoked salmon. Cover with plastic wrap and refrigerate overnight.

Preheat oven to 350°F (180°C).

To remove the smoked salmon from the terrine, place the entire terrine in the oven for 2–3 minutes, then remove it and turn it out onto a cutting surface. Give the terrine a little shake and gently lift off the mold. Slice and serve.

MAKES ONE 12-INCH (30-CM) TERRINE

SERVES 12 OR 24 HORS D'OEUVRES

Ingredients

12		**fingerling potatoes, blanched and halved**
1		**fennel bulb, julienned**
2		**carrots, peeled and julienned**
2 lbs. · 1 kg		**salmon fillets cut into 6 portions**
		kosher salt and white pepper to taste
3		**lemons, sectioned, juice reserved**
½ cup · 125 mL		**butter, cut into 6 pieces**
½ cup · 125 mL		**chives, finely chopped**
½ cup · 125 mL		**sparkling wine**

Fillet of Salmon
Baked in Parchment with Sparkling Wine

Cooking in parchment paper is a well-established technique in haute cuisine. The French term en papillote *refers to a specific method whereby the food is placed in a parchment parcel. As the food bakes and lets off steam, the paper bubbles up into an attractive dome. At the table, the paper is slit open to release the aroma.*

Preheat oven to 400°F (200°C).

Lay six 12-inch (30-cm) squares of parchment paper or foil on a countertop. On the bottom third of each square place 4 pieces of blanched fingerling potatoes, cut sides facing down. Divide the fennel and carrot into small piles on top of the potatoes. Arrange the salmon on top of the vegetables and season with salt and pepper to taste.

Distribute the lemon sections, butter and chives evenly over each piece of salmon. Pour equal amounts of the sparkling wine over top each piece of salmon. Fold the parchment paper over and seal the edges by rolling them tightly. With the palm of your hand, press down on the rolled up seal to keep it from unraveling.

Place the fish parcels on a baking sheet and bake for 10 minutes. Serve immediately, opening the parcels at the table.

MAKES 6 SERVINGS

Ingredients

2 Tbsp. • 30 mL		**olive oil**
2 lbs. • 1 kg		**rainbow trout fillets, pin bones removed, cut into 6 portions**
		kosher salt and white pepper to taste
2 Tbsp. • 30 mL		**unsalted butter**
1		**shallot, finely diced**
1		**leek (white part only), finely diced**
2		**tomato, seeded and finely chopped**
1 cup • 250 mL		**35% cream**
1		**lemon, juice of**
1 cup • 250 mL		**seedless grapes, halved**
$\frac{1}{4}$ cup • 50 mL		**sparkling wine**

NOTE

If you are not serving the sauce immediately, keep it warm and add the wine only at the last moment when it's needed.

Rainbow Trout
with Sparkling Wine, Grape and Cream Sauce

The grapes in this recipe reinforce the fresh fruit flavor of sparkling wine. When combined with cream and grapes, the gentle acidity of the wine enhances the flavor of the rainbow trout. Adding sparkling wine to the sauce at the last moment preserves its delicate structure and the bubbles add lightness to the dish.

Heat a large sauté pan, add the olive oil and heat. Season the trout with salt and pepper. Add the trout to the hot oil, flesh-side down, and sauté for 3 minutes until golden brown. Turn the fish over to the skin side and reduce the heat to moderate. Cook for another 3 minutes. Carefully remove the trout from the sauté pan and keep warm.

In a small saucepot, heat the butter until it foams. Add the shallot and leek and cook until soft, stirring frequently for 3 to 5 minutes to avoid any coloring. Add the tomato and cream and season with salt and pepper. Bring the cream to a boil, reduce the heat to a gentle simmer for 10 minutes or until the cream has thickened enough to coat the back of a spoon. Add the lemon juice and grapes then readjust the seasoning.

Add the sparkling wine to the sauce. Stir just before serving. Transfer the warm trout to dinner plates and spoon over the grape sauce. Serve immediately to preserve the bubbles in the sauce.

MAKES 6 SERVINGS

Pickerel in Saffron
and Sparkling Wine Broth

This recipe is ideal for taking advantage of the beautiful lake fish available during the summer months. The delicate nature of pickerel calls for a light preparation. Harmonize the flavors by cooking with the same wine you intend to drink.

Ingredients

2 lbs. ·	1 kg	**fresh pickerel fillets, pin bones removed, cut into 6 portions**
2 Tbsp. ·	30 mL	**unsalted butter**
2 Tbsp. ·	30 mL	**olive oil**
		kosher salt and white pepper to taste

Rub the flesh side of the pickerel with butter and drizzle olive oil over the fillets. Season with salt and pepper. Roll each fish fillet from tail to head, secure with a toothpick then refrigerate until needed.

MAKES 6 SERVINGS

recipe continued on next page

Ingredients

¼ cup	· 50 mL	**olive oil**
2		**shallots, peeled and thinly sliced**
1		**leek (white part only), washed and chopped**
4		**white mushrooms, cleaned and chopped**
1		**ripe tomato, chopped**
1 Tbsp.	· 15 mL	**ginger, peeled and finely chopped**
1 stalk		**lemon grass, crushed**
pinch		**saffron**
1 cup	· 250 mL	**sparkling wine**
4 cups	· 1 L	**Chicken Stock (page 267)**
2 Tbsp.	· 30 mL	**lime juice**

Sparkling Wine Broth

Heat a large soup pot over medium heat and add the olive oil. Add the shallots, leek and mushrooms and cook for 5 minutes, stirring frequently until the vegetables soften. Add the tomato, ginger and lemon grass and continue cooking for 10 minutes until the vegetables have softened and become translucent. Add the saffron, sparkling wine and stock and bring to a boil.

Reduce the heat to a simmer and cook for 45 minutes. Strain the liquid and discard the solids. Transfer the stock to a smaller pot and bring to a simmer. Reduce the stock until only 1 cup (250 mL) remains. Add the lime juice and keep warm.

Ingredients

½ cup	•	125 mL	**snow peas, blanched and julienned**
¼ cup	•	50 mL	**butternut squash, blanched and julienned**
1			**carrot, blanched and julienned**
¼ cup	•	50 mL	**rutabaga, blanched and julienned**
1			**red onion, julienned**
¼ cup	•	50 mL	**savoy cabbage, blanched and julienned**
1			**leek (white part only), blanched and julienned**
2 cups	•	500 mL	**Sparkling Wine Broth (page 26)**
2 Tbsp.	•	30 mL	**unsalted butter, cubed**
1 tsp.	•	5 mL	**thyme, finely chopped**
			kosher salt and white pepper to taste

for the garnish

Preheat the oven to 375°F (190°C).

Combine the blanched vegetables with the Sparkling Wine Broth and bring to a simmer over medium heat.

Remove the fish from the refrigerator and place in an oven-proof dish. Place in the oven and cook for 10 minutes.

Stir the butter and thyme into the warm stock and vegetables. Remove the fish from the oven. Using a slotted spoon, divide the vegetables among 6 large bowls. Place the cooked pickerel over the vegetables and pour the saffron sparkling wine broth over top. Serve immediately.

Ingredients

1 Tbsp.	• 15 mL	**honey**
2 Tbsp.	• 30 mL	**olive oil**
2 tsp.	• 10 mL	**sesame oil**
4		**garlic cloves, crushed, and finely chopped**
1 Tbsp.	• 15 mL	**fresh ginger, finely chopped**
2		**jalapeño chili, finely chopped**
2		**limes, juice and zest of**
1 Tbsp.	• 15 mL	**coriander, finely chopped**
4 Tbsp.	• 60 mL	**rice wine vinegar**
2 Tbsp.	• 30 mL	**sweet chili sauce**
4 Tbsp.	• 60 mL	**dark soy sauce**
pinch		**turmeric**
30		**black tiger shrimp, jumbo size, peeled and deveined**
6		**lemon grass stalks, outer skins removed**
		kosher salt and white pepper to taste

Lemon Grass Shrimp Skewers

I first made this dish when I was the executive chef of Taboo Restaurant in Toronto in the early 1990s. I was then asked to make an appearance live on CTV's "Eye on Toronto" show. During the rush of the live demonstration, I forgot a tray of shrimp in the oven and remembered only as I was driving home. I was never invited back!

Combine all the ingredients, except the shrimp and lemon grass, in a glass bowl. Add the shrimp. Stir to combine and refrigerate for 1 hour.

Preheat the grill to medium-high.

Using a sharp knife, cut points on the ends of each lemon grass stalk. Skewer each shrimp (5 per lemon grass stalk) by running the lemon grass stalk from the tail end to the head so that each shrimp is in a letter "U" position. Season the shrimp with salt and pepper. Grill until the shrimp have turned pink and are cooked through, about 5 minutes per side. Serve with your favorite risotto.

MAKES 6 SERVINGS

Ingredients

1 cup	•	250 mL	**baby frisée lettuce**
1 cup	•	250 mL	**red leaf lettuce**
1 cup	•	250 mL	**green leaf lettuce**
2			**apples, cored and thinly sliced**
$\frac{1}{4}$ cup	•	50 mL	**lightly toasted walnut halves**
$\frac{1}{2}$ cup	•	125 mL	**sweet red pepper, roasted, peeled and julienned**
$\frac{1}{4}$ cup	•	50 mL	**crumbled blue cheese (optional)**
6 Tbsp.	•	90 mL	**aged balsamic vinegar**
6 Tbsp.	•	90 mL	**extra virgin olive oil**
4 tsp.	•	20 mL	**mint, finely chopped**
4 tsp.	•	20 mL	**basil, finely chopped**
36			**very thin slices duck prosciutto**
			kosher salt and white pepper to taste

Duck Prosciutto Salad
with Celery Root Remoulade

Clearly inspired by the famous Waldorf salad, this version combines a few of my favorite fall flavors. Celery root is an under-utilized vegetable with deep flavor and crunch. The addition of thinly sliced duck prosciutto makes this appetizer an interesting match for sparkling wine.

Combine the 3 lettuces and divide among 6 large plates.

Combine the remaining ingredients, except for the duck prosciutto, in a large salad bowl, tossing gently. Season with salt and pepper.

Divide the salad into 6 portions atop the lettuce. Top each salad with 6 slices of duck prosciutto (see page 32). Garnish with celery root remoulade (next page).

MAKES 6 SERVINGS
recipe continued on next two pages

Ingredients

1 cup	• 250 mL	**celery root, julienned**
1		**lemon, juice of**
		kosher salt and white pepper to taste
1 Tbsp.	• 15 mL	**Dijon mustard**
2 Tbsp.	• 30 mL	**chives, finely diced**
2 Tbsp.	• 30 mL	**mayonnaise (page 13)**

Celery Root Remoulade

A remoulade sauce is classically prepared with mayonnaise, capers, gherkins and anchovies. In this recipe, the capers, anchovies and gherkins are replaced by the celery root, mustard and lemon juice for a less sharp but equally delicious condiment specifically dressed for the duck prosciutto, apple and walnut salad.

Combine all of the ingredients and allow to marinate for 24 hours in the refrigerator, covered with plastic wrap to prevent discoloration.

Ingredients

1 cup	•	250 mL	**sugar**
1 cup	•	250 mL	**kosher salt**
2			**bay leaves**
2 sprigs			**thyme, finely chopped**
1 sprig			**rosemary, finely chopped**
2 tsp.	•	10 mL	**juniper berries, crushed**
1 Tbsp.	•	15 mL	**crushed black pepper**
2			**whole duck breasts, trimmed of sinew**

Homemade Duck Prosciutto

A NOTE ON CURED MEATS

Home-curing meats can be a wonder-fully rewarding experience when conducted with the utmost care. If not done correctly, you could be exposed to serious foodborne illness such as botulism and salmonella. Please follow the recipe very care-fully and if at any time in the curing process the item being cured develops unpleasant odors and/or mold, please discard it immediately.

Combine the sugar and salt with the bay leaves, thyme, rose-mary, juniper berries and black pepper. Place the duck breast in a small casserole with the skin side down and completely cover the duck with the sugar/salt mixture. Place in the refrigerator, covered, and let cure for 36 hours.

Remove the duck from the cure and rinse under cold water. Pat dry with kitchen towel and refrigerate the duck breast overnight, unwrapped. Wrap the duck breast tightly in cheese-cloth and place in a cool, dark and well-ventilated storage area for 3 months. Remove the cheesecloth wrapping from the duck. Slice thinly and serve.

$\frac{1}{4}$ cup	•	50 mL	**olive oil**
2 Tbsp.	•	30 mL	**duck fat from the duck confit**
1			**onion, finely chopped**
2			**cloves garlic, finely chopped**
1			**carrot, peeled and finely chopped**
1			**leek (white part only), finely chopped**
1			**celery stalk, finely chopped**
3 oz.	•	75 g	**prosciutto, finely chopped**
1 lb.	•	500 g	**du Puy (green) lentils**
3			**tomatoes, seeded and chopped**
10 cups	•	2.25 L	**Chicken Stock (page 267)**
1 Tbsp.	•	15 mL	**rosemary, finely chopped**
1 Tbsp.	•	15 mL	**thyme, finely chopped**
			kosher salt and white pepper to taste
2 Tbsp.	•	30 mL	**sherry vinegar**
2 cups	•	500 mL	**Duck Confit (page 34)**

Lentil Soup
with Duck Confit

This robust, delicious and satisfying soup is suited to a wine that is rich and full flavored, such as an earthy Pinot Noir, or even a Merlot or Cabernet Sauvignon. However, I have included it here to showcase sparkling wine's amazing ability to cleanse the palate and revive the taste buds. Rich, fatty and salty foods are a natural choice when drinking sparkling wine.

In a soup pot set over moderate heat sauté the olive oil, duck fat, onion and garlic for 2 minutes, stirring frequently. Add the carrot, leek, celery and prosciutto and sauté until the vegetables and prosciutto are slightly browned.

Meanwhile, rinse the lentils under cold water and drain. Add the lentils and tomatoes to the vegetables and stir to combine. Add the stock and bring to a boil. Reduce the heat to a simmer and cook, uncovered, for 45 minutes or until the lentils are tender. Remove the soup from the heat.

Using a slotted spoon, remove 2 cups/500 mL of the lentils from the soup and reserve. Transfer the remaining soup to a food processor and purée until smooth. Return the puréed lentil soup to the pot over medium heat and bring the soup to a simmer. Add the chopped herbs and season with salt, pepper and vinegar.

Combine the reserved lentils with the reserved duck confit. Pour the soup into 6 warmed soup bowls. Garnish with the lentil and confit mixture.

MAKES 6 SERVINGS

recipe continued on next page

Ingredients

1 cup	•	250 mL	**coarse salt**
$\frac{1}{2}$ cup	•	125 mL	**granulated sugar**
2 Tbsp.	•	30 mL	**coarsely ground black pepper**
1 Tbsp.	•	15 mL	**garlic, thinly sliced**
1 Tbsp.	•	15 mL	**ginger, finely chopped**
2			**duck legs**
3 cups	•	750 mL	**duck fat**

Duck Confit

Combine all the ingredients except the duck legs and duck fat. Rub the duck legs with the salt mixture to cover thoroughly. Pack tightly in a small container, cover with plastic wrap and marinate for 3 days in the refrigerator.

Preheat oven to 300°F (150°C).

Rinse the salt marinade off the duck legs under a stream of cold water and pat dry. Place the duck legs in an ovenproof pot. Cover the legs with the duck fat and cover with a lid. Bake the duck confit for 2–3 hours or until the meat is fork tender and easily pulled away from the bone.

When the confit is cool, pick the meat off the bones and discard the bones. Tear the meat into bite-size pieces. Reserve at room temperature to be used in the soup. When the duck fat is cool, strain it through a sieve and refrigerate.

Ingredients

2 Tbsp.	·	30 mL	**unsalted butter at room temperature**
2 Tbsp.	·	30 mL	**grated Parmesan cheese**
6 oz.	·	170 g	**grated aged cheddar**
2 Tbsp.	·	30 mL	**rosemary, finely chopped**
1 recipe			**soufflé base (page 37)**
6			**egg whites**

Aged Cheddar and Rosemary Soufflé

A warm soufflé is the perfect meal on a cool autumn day. Make this recipe in two parts and be sure to thoroughly chill the soufflé base before adding the cheddar and the rosemary. Serve the soufflé as an appetizer or an entrée. A fruity sparkling wine with good acidity is the perfect way to enjoy this soufflé; the crispness of the wine and the pungency of the aged cheddar are in perfect contrast.

Preheat oven to 425°F (220°C).

Rub the inside of six 6-inch (10-cm) ramekins with butter and a sprinkling of Parmesan.

In a large bowl combine the cheddar, rosemary and soufflé base.

In a separate bowl, beat the egg whites to soft peaks. Fold about one-third of the egg whites into the base. Add the remaining whites in two more additions. Spoon the soufflé batter into the prepared ramekins to within 1 inch (2.5 cm) of the rims. Wipe the rims and gently tap the ramekins on the counter to settle the batter. Bake for 16–18 minutes or until golden brown and cooked through. Serve immediately.

MAKES 6 SERVINGS

Ingredients

¹/₄ cup	50 mL	**unsalted butter**
3 Tbsp.	45 mL	**all-purpose flour**
1¹/₂ cups	375 mL	**whole milk**
		kosher salt and white pepper to taste
10		**egg yolks**

for the soufflé base

Melt the butter in a pan over low heat then add the flour. Stir frequently for 8 to 10 minutes to cook the flour, making a roux.

In another small pan, heat the milk just until it begins to steam. Slowly add the hot milk to the roux in small batches, whisking vigorously and frequently until the mix is very smooth. Add salt and pepper to taste.

Place the egg yolks in a stainless steel bowl and add 3 Tbsp. (45 mL) of the hot soufflé base mix. Stir quickly until well combined. Using a rubber spatula, scrape the eggs into the pot with the soufflé base mix. Stir to combine.

It is important not to let the mixture boil or the eggs will scramble, so simmer at a very low temperature. Season with salt and pepper. Remove from the heat and let cool to room temperature. Refrigerate until ready to use.

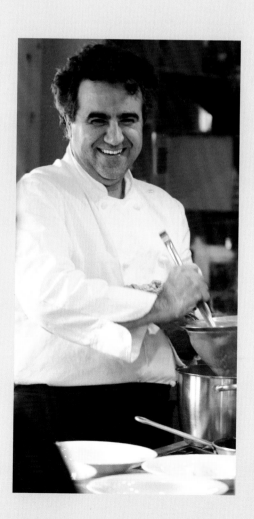

Wine Country Duck Burger

This burger is like no other. Believe me. Serve a small burger as an appetizer at an elegant fall dinner party and your guests will be asking you for your autograph. It's not inexpensive to prepare because the ingredients are premium, but if it's something memorable you want, then you must try it.

Ingredients

1 cup	•	250 mL	**crustless white bread, cubed**
¼ cup	•	50 mL	**cold Chicken Stock (page 267)**
1 lb.	•	500 g	**duck meat, cubed**
4 oz.	•	125 g	**ground pork loin, cubed**
1			**egg**
2 tsp.	•	10 mL	**ginger, peeled and minced**
1 tsp.	•	5 mL	**coriander seeds, toasted and ground**
2 tsp.	•	10 mL	**sesame seeds, toasted**
2 cloves			**garlic, minced**
1 Tbsp.	•	15 mL	**fresh rosemary, finely chopped**
2 oz.	•	50 g	**prosciutto, finely diced**
2			**shallots, finely diced**
2 tsp.	•	10 mL	**cracked black pepper**
			kosher salt and white pepper to taste
2 oz.	•	50 g	**blue cheese**

Combine the bread with the chicken stock. Pass the bread, duck and pork through the largest holes of a meat grinder. Refrigerate until thoroughly chilled.

Pass the chilled meat/bread mixture through the medium holes of a meat grinder. Refrigerate until thoroughly chilled once again.

Transfer the meat to the chilled bowl of a food processor (or stand mixer) and add the egg, ginger, coriander, sesame seeds, garlic, rosemary, prosciutto, shallots and cracked black pepper. Mix on low speed until thoroughly combined. Season with salt and pepper.

(To test seasoning, pinch off a piece of the burger and sauté in a small frying pan with a touch of olive oil. Once cooked through, taste it and make any desired adjustments.)

Add the blue cheese and mix on low speed until just combined. Remove the burger mix from the bowl and refrigerate for 3 hours.

Remove the burger mix from the refrigerator and shape into 6 burgers. Refrigerate once more until ready to cook.

Preheat the grill to medium high. Place burgers on the grill and cook to desired doneness. Remove from the grill and serve.

MAKES 6 BURGERS

Ingredients

¼ cup	•	50 mL	**olive oil**
¼ cup	•	50 mL	**unsalted butter**
2			**onions, finely chopped**
2 tsp.	•	10 mL	**garlic, finely chopped**
4 sprigs			**fresh thyme, finely chopped**
2 sprigs			**fresh rosemary, finely chopped**
1 Tbsp.	•	15 mL	**crushed black pepper**
¼ cup	•	50 mL	**brandy**
¼ cup	•	50 mL	**Madeira**
2 cups	•	500 mL	**35% cream**
7			**whole eggs**
7			**egg yolks**
2 Tbsp.	•	30 mL	**granulated sugar**
2 Tbsp.	•	30 mL	**kosher salt**
2½ lb.	•	1.2 kg	**chicken livers**

Windsor Arms Creamy Liver Pâté

In 1992 I was hired as the executive chef of the Millcroft Inn. This Relais and Châteaux property was owned and managed by George Minden. Mr. Minden also owned the Windsor Arms Hotel. This pâté was served in both restaurants and I am not sure which chef actually created the recipe. It was a menu item I could never remove because whenever I tried to guests would write letters of complaint.

In a large sauté pan over high heat add the olive oil and the butter. When the butter is frothy, add the onions and sauté, stirring frequently, until golden brown. Add the garlic, thyme and rosemary and stir to incorporate. Add the brandy and Madeira and carefully set the alcohol alight. When the flame subsides, reduce the heat and simmer until only 2 Tbsp. (30 mL) of liquid remains in the pan. Remove from the heat and cool to room temperature.

Preheat oven to 300°F (150°C).

Transfer half the browned onions to a food processor. Add half the chicken livers. Combine the cream with the eggs, eggs yolks, sugar and salt and add half this mix to the food processor. Purée until smooth. Pour out into a clean bowl and repeat with the remaining ingredients. Pass the pâté through a medium sieve. Pour the pâté into an ovenproof casserole and place in a bain-marie.

Cover with aluminum foil and bake for 2–3 hours or until an internal temperature of 160°F (85°C) is reached.

Remove from the oven and cool to room temperature. Remove the foil and cover with plastic wrap. Refrigerate overnight to set. To serve, use a warmed tablespoon to scoop out the pâté.

MAKES 8 CUPS /2 L

Ingredients

¼ cup · 50 mL		**olive oil**
¼ cup · 50 mL		**unsalted butter**
1		**onion, finely chopped**
1		**leek (white part only), finely chopped**
¼ bulb		**fennel, finely chopped**
1		**carrot, peeled and finely chopped**
3 cups · 750 mL		**squash (such as butternut, acorn or buttercup), peeled and coarsely chopped)**
2 cloves		**garlic, finely chopped**
1 Tbsp. · 15 mL		**ginger, peeled and finely chopped**
½ tsp. · 2 mL		**allspice**
½ tsp. · 2 mL		**cloves**
½ tsp. · 2 mL		**nutmeg**
2		**star anise**
1 stick		**cinnamon**
8 cups · 2 L		**Mushroom Vegetable Stock (page 43)**
		kosher salt and white pepper to taste
36		**oysters, washed and scrubbed**
½ cup · 125 mL		**buttermilk**

Harvest Squash Soup
with Buttermilk and Oysters

This soup is the perfect antidote to a long cold winter. The flavors of squash are comforting, but when it's simmered with the harvest spices and garnished with fresh oysters, you may wish that winter would never end.

Place a large soup pot over medium-high heat and add the olive oil and butter. When the butter is frothy, add the onion, leek and fennel. Sauté, stirring frequently, until the vegetables are soft but not colored. Add the squash, carrot, garlic and ginger and stir to combine. Cook for 5 minutes then add the allspice, cloves, nutmeg, star anise and cinnamon. Stir to combine and cook the spices for 10 minutes longer, stirring frequently.

Add the stock and bring to a boil. Reduce the heat to a simmer. Continue cooking for 45 minutes or until the vegetables have cooked through. Remove the soup from the heat and strain through a colander into another pot. Reserve the liquid.

Transfer the contents of the colander to a food processor and purée until smooth. Place the puréed solids into a clean soup pot and add enough of the reserved stock to make a smooth soup. Bring the soup to a simmer and season with salt and pepper.

A NOTE ON USING BUTTERMILK

Once the buttermilk has been added do not let the soup boil or it will curdle. Also, you can vary the degree of thickness by adding more or less soup liquid to the purée in the pan. Just make sure it comes back to a simmer. You can also add a little more buttermilk for a slightly more sour taste.

In the meantime, shuck the oysters, discard the shells and reserve the juice.

Add the buttermilk to the soup and immediately turn off the heat. Divide the soup among 6 warm soup bowls. Top each with 6 oysters and serve immediately.

MAKES 6 SERVINGS

Ingredients

2 Tbsp. ·	30 mL	**olive oil**
2 Tbsp. ·	30 mL	**unsalted butter**
2		**onions, chopped**
1		**leek (white part only), washed and chopped**
2		**carrots, peeled and chopped**
2 stalks		**celery, chopped**
2 cloves		**garlic, chopped**
2 lbs. ·	1 kg	**mushrooms**
2 cups ·	500 mL	**white wine**
16 cups ·	4 L	**water**
1		**bouquet garni (page 241)**

Mushroom Vegetable Stock

This is a versatile stock that can be made with different combinations of seasonal vegetables and flavorings. By using a variety of seasonal mushrooms, you will ensure a full-flavored stock suitable for many recipes.

In a large stockpot set over medium heat, warm the olive oil and butter. When the butter is frothy, add the onions and leeks. Cook for a few minutes until the onions are soft. Add the carrots, celery and garlic. Cook for 5 minutes more, stirring frequently, then add the mushrooms. Sauté for a few minutes, stirring frequently, then add the wine and water. Bring to a gentle simmer and add the bouquet garni.

Simmer for 2 hours, occasionally skimming the surface of the stock to remove impurities.

Pass the stock through a sieve and refrigerate until required.

MAKES 12 CUPS /3 L

Ingredients

12 oz.	•	375 g	**duck foie gras, divided into 6 portions**
			kosher salt and white pepper to taste
2 Tbsp.	•	30 mL	**unsalted butter**
4			**fingerling potatoes, halved and blanched**
1 cup	•	250 mL	**whole blanched almonds**
³⁄₄ cup	•	175 mL	**dried apricots, diced**
½ cup	•	125 mL	**Riesling icewine**
½ cup	•	125 mL	**beets, cooked and cubed**

Foie Gras with Icewine, Almond
and Dried Apricot Sauté

Foie gras is the fattened liver of duck or goose. It is very expensive and can be difficult to work with, but if you are looking for a recipe to suit a very special dinner, then it may be worth it. In this recipe, Riesling icewine provides the base for a delicious combination of foie gras, dried apricots and almonds.

Using the tip of a small sharp knife, score each piece of foie gras on both sides. Sprinkle each piece with salt and pepper and refrigerate.

Add the butter to a sauté pan set over medium heat. When the butter is frothy, add the potatoes and cook, stirring frequently, until they are golden brown. Remove the potatoes from the pan. Add the almonds and cook for a few minutes until they become golden brown.

Return the potatoes to the pan and add the dried apricots and the icewine. Bring to a simmer and reduce until the icewine has become quite syrupy, about 20 minutes. In a separate saucepan, heat the beets until warmed through then reserve. Cook the foie gras on high heat until golden brown on each side.

Remove the foie gras to a kitchen towel to absorb excess grease.

Divide the potato/apricot sauté among 6 plates. Top each plate with a slice of foie gras and sprinkle the beets around the edges. Serve immediately.

MAKES 6 SERVINGS

Ingredients

¼ cup	• 50 mL	**olive oil**
2 Tbsp.	• 30 mL	**unsalted butter**
3 lbs.	• 1.5 kg	**sea scallops**
		kosher salt and white pepper to taste

Scallops with Crab
on Basil Brut Syrup

One of the most popular events at Hillebrand Estates Winery Restaurant is our icewine makers' dinner held every January. A few years ago we created a cocktail called the Golden Brut, which is a nicely balanced blend of sparkling wine and icewine.

Heat a heavy-bottomed sauté pan over medium-high heat. Add the olive oil and butter and when the butter is frothy add the scallops. Cook the scallops until golden brown on one side, 3–5 minutes. Turn the scallops over and brown the other side for 1–2 minutes. Remove the scallops from the heat and keep warm.

Reserve the pan for the next step.

MAKES 6 SERVINGS
recipe continued on next page

Ingredients

$\frac{1}{4}$ cup	· 50 mL	**unsalted butter**
$\frac{1}{2}$ cup	· 125 mL	**fingerling potatoes, blanched**
$\frac{1}{2}$ cup	· 125 mL	**icewine**
$\frac{1}{2}$ cup	· 125 mL	**sparkling wine**
		kosher salt and white pepper to taste
6		**leaves fresh basil, torn in small pieces**

for the sauté

Add the butter to the same pan that you used to sear the scallops. When the butter is frothy, add the potatoes and sauté until golden brown, stirring frequently. Add the icewine and the sparkling wine and simmer until reduced to a maple syrup consistency. Season with salt and pepper to taste. Add the basil and keep warm.

Ingredients

$\frac{1}{2}$ lb.	· 250 g	**crabmeat**
2 Tbsp.	· 30 mL	**red pepper, seeded and finely diced**
2 Tbsp.	· 30 mL	**red onion, finely diced**
1 Tbsp.	· 15 mL	**green onion, finely diced**
2 tsp.	· 10 mL	**chives, minced**
1		**lemon, juice and zest of**
$\frac{1}{4}$ cup	· 50 mL	**bread crumbs**
$\frac{1}{4}$ cup	· 50 mL	**sour cream**
		kosher salt and white pepper to taste
1 Tbsp.	· 15 mL	**coriander, finely chopped**
pinch		**cayenne pepper**

for the crab salad

Preheat oven to 375°F (190°C).

Combine the crabmeat with the rest of the ingredients and mix well. Taste and adjust the seasoning. Place a small dollop of crab on each scallop then heat the scallops in the oven for 3–5 minutes.

Divide the potato basil sauté among 6 warm dinner plates. Remove the scallops from the oven and place on top of the sauté. Spoon around some icewine syrup and serve immediately.

MAKES 6 SERVINGS

Ingredients

1			**vanilla pod, split and quartered**
¹⁄₂ cup	•	125 mL	**icewine**
¹⁄₂ cup	•	125 mL	**sparkling wine**
2 tsp.	•	10 mL	**crushed black pepper**
2 lbs.	•	1 kg	**Arctic char fillets, divided into 6 portions**
2 Tbsp.	•	30 mL	**unsalted butter**
2 Tbsp.	•	30 mL	**olive oil**

Vanilla-Cured Arctic Char
with Winter Greens and Barley Risotto

At the 2003 icewine makers' dinner, Hillebrand's wine maker, J.L. Groux, challenged me to prepare a menu with icewine in every course. I decided to take advantage of the relatively high acidity found in a 1999 bottle of Vidal icewine. I realized that this acidity could actually lightly "cure" a delicate fish fillet, imparting the fruity intensity of the icewine.

Preheat oven to 350°F (180°C).

In a small bowl combine the vanilla pod, icewine, sparkling wine and black pepper. Place the fish fillets in an ovenproof casserole with the skin side up and pour over the vanilla marinade. Refrigerate the fish overnight, turning the fillets every so often.

Remove the fish from the marinade and pat dry with paper towel. Discard the marinade.

Add the butter and olive oil to a moderately hot non-stick sauté pan. When the butter is frothy add the char and sauté skin-side down for 3 minutes. Turn the fish over and turn off the heat. Keep warm.

MAKES 6 SERVINGS

recipe continued on next three pages

Ingredients

1 cup	• 250 mL	**Fish Stock (page 50)**
1 cup	• 250 mL	**cooked barley**
½ cup	• 125 mL	**Butternut Squash Purée (page 51)**
		kosher salt and white pepper to taste
2 Tbsp.	• 30 mL	**unsalted butter**
2 Tbsp.	• 30 mL	**grated Parmesan cheese**
1 cup	• 250 mL	**winter greens, such as Swiss chard**
½ cup	• 125 mL	**sparkling wine**

Winter Greens and Barley Risotto

In a medium saucepan combine the fish stock and the cooked barley. Bring to a boil then reduce heat to a gentle simmer. When the stock has evaporated and the barley has thickened, about 15 minutes, add the butternut squash purée and stir to incorporate. Season to taste with salt and pepper. Add the butter and the Parmesan. Add the winter greens and stir to combine until the butter has melted. Add the sparkling wine and stir to incorporate. Serve immediately with the icewine-cured Arctic char.

Ingredients

$\frac{1}{4}$ cup	· 50 mL	**unsalted butter**
$\frac{1}{2}$ bulb		**fennel, chopped**
1		**onion, chopped**
2		**leeks (white part only), washed and chopped**
2 lbs.	· 1 kg	**fish bones, from white fish only, rinsed**
8 cups	· 2L	**cold water**
2 cups	· 500 mL	**white wine**
1		**lemon, sliced**
3 sprigs		**parsley**
2 sprigs		**thyme**
1		**bay leaf**
2		**star anise**

Fish Stock

In a small soup pot set over medium heat melt the butter and add the fennel, onion and leeks. Sauté the vegetables for about 5 minutes, stirring frequently until soft. Add the fish bones and cold water to cover the bones entirely. Bring to a simmer and add the wine, lemon, herbs and spices.

Simmer for 2 hours. Strain though a fine sieve and refrigerate until required.

MAKES 8 CUPS / 2 L

Ingredients

2 Tbsp. · 30 mL		olive oil
2 Tbsp. · 30 mL		butter
$\frac{1}{2}$ cup · 125 mL		onion, peeled and finely chopped
$\frac{1}{2}$ cup · 125 mL		fennel, finely chopped
1		leek (white part only), chopped
2 cloves		garlic, peeled and minced
2 cups · 500 mL		butternut squash, peeled and roughly chopped
1 tsp. · 5 mL		mild paprika
$\frac{1}{2}$ tsp. · 2 mL		cayenne pepper (more or less to taste)
1		bay leaf
$\frac{1}{2}$ cup · 125 mL		dry white wine
2 cups · 500 mL		chicken stock
1 tsp. · 5 mL		white wine vinegar
		kosher salt and white pepper to taste

Butternut Squash Purée

In a large stockpot, heat the oil to moderately high and add the butter. When the butter is frothy, add in the onion, fennel and leek and cook for 10 minutes, stirring frequently. Add the garlic and butternut squash.

Stir frequently for 5 minutes, then add the paprika, cayenne pepper and the bay leaf. Add the white wine and the chicken stock. Bring to a boil.

Reduce heat and simmer for 35–45 minutes or until all the vegetables are cooked through. Transfer to a food processor and purée. Strain the purée through a sieve into a bowl.

Add the white wine vinegar, season to taste and reserve until required.

MAKES 4 CUPS / 1 L

Spring

Asparagus Bisque
  with Fancy Potato Chips

Pizza of Asparagus,
  Morels and Prosciutto

Goat Cheese and Sauvignon Blanc
  Terrine with Dried Fruit

Lollipops

Summer

Tomatoes Stuffed
  with Fava Beans and Goat Cheese

Poached Pickerel
  with Watercress Sauce

Asparagus Scallop Salad
  with Leeks and
  Sweet and Sour Dressing

Artichoke Tapenade

Spiked Gazpacho

Sauvignon

SAUVIGNON BLANC IS ONE OF MY FAVORITE VARIETALS. THIS grape produces wines of medium body and it can accommodate and pair well with a broad range of flavors, including herbal and grassy to exotic fruit. It also produces wines with very interesting bouquets, from echoes of passion fruit, lychee nuts, gooseberry, papaya and pineapple, to herbaceous and straw. With flavor profiles such as this, is it any wonder that Sauvignon Blanc is a wonderful wine for matching with food?

Sauvignon Blanc's generous acidity makes it a perfect palate cleanser, which makes it a nice match for foods that might be too strong in character for other wines such as the Rieslings or Chardonnays. I call Sauvignon

Autumn

Gingered Carrot and Apple Soup

**Harvest Beets and Goat Cheese
with Pumpkin Sauvignon Blanc
Vinaigrette**

Vegetable Burgers

Winter

Jerusalem Artichoke Soup

**Chicken Liver Vegetable Pâté
with Quince Marmalade**

**Atlantic Sea Scallops
with Vegetable Tempura**

**Chicken Legs
Marinated in Yogurt and Lime**

Blanc

Blanc my "asparagus" wine because I find a nice dry Sauvignon Blanc's grassy character matches well with my asparagus recipes.

This wine can be served as an aperitif or paired with food of medium body. We have often paired Sauvignon Blanc with goat cheese appetizers, vegetable-based soups and our famous asparagus and morel mushroom pizza. I would recommend a fresh and fruity Sauvignon Blanc in the spring and summer to refresh your palate and quench your thirst. In the fall I would choose a herbaceous wine, perhaps one that has been barrel-aged for a short period. Either way, the joys of Sauvignon Blanc can be discovered on their own or with interesting menu items. The only way to be certain which style you prefer is to be adventurous. And there's plenty of opportunity for adventure in my wine country cuisine.

Ingredients

2 Tbsp.	·	30 mL	**olive oil**
2 Tbsp.	·	30 mL	**butter**
$\frac{1}{2}$ cup	·	125 mL	**onion, chopped**
2			**leeks (white part only), chopped**
2 cups	·	500 mL	**potato, peeled and cubed**
2 cloves			**garlic, minced**
1 tsp.	·	5 mL	**mild paprika**
$\frac{1}{2}$ tsp.	·	2 mL	**cayenne pepper**
1			**bay leaf**
$\frac{1}{2}$ cup	·	125 mL	**dry white wine**
6 cups	·	1.5 L	**Chicken Stock (page 267)**
3 Tbsp.	·	45 mL	**olive oil**
3 cups	·	750 mL	**asparagus, peeled and chopped**
$\frac{1}{2}$ cup	·	125 mL	**35% cream**
1 tsp.	·	5 mL	**white wine vinegar**
			kosher salt and white pepper to taste

Asparagus Bisque
with Fancy Potato Chips

When the first asparagus comes into season there can be no mistaking its effect on my kitchen. No other event at any other time of the year is as uplifting and rejuvenating as the first asparagus. After a long winter, a bowl of this soup garnished simply with some homemade potato chips is satisfying, and I dare you to eat a bowl of asparagus soup in May without smiling between mouthfuls.

In a large soup pot, heat the 2 Tbsp. (30 mL) oil to moderately high and add the butter. When the butter is frothy, add the onion, leeks and potato and cook for 10 minutes, stirring frequently, until the vegetables have softened. Add the garlic and stir frequently for 5 minutes, then add the paprika, cayenne and bay leaf. Add the white wine and the chicken stock. Bring to a rapid boil, reduce the heat and simmer for 35 to 45 minutes or until the vegetables are cooked through.

Meanwhile, in a separate pan heat the 3 Tbsp. (45 mL) olive oil and add the asparagus. Stir frequently to avoid browning as the asparagus becomes soft and tender. When the asparagus is cooked through, about 20 minutes, add it to the soup pot and stir to blend with the other ingredients. Transfer the soup to a food processor and purée. Strain through a sieve into a clean soup pot.

Add the cream and return the soup to a boil. Reduce heat, add the vinegar and the salt and pepper to taste. Keep the soup warm.

MAKES 8 SERVINGS

recipe continued on next page

Ingredients

2 cups · 500 mL   **vegetable oil**

1   **potato, peeled**

                     sea salt to taste

Fancy Potato Chips

Pour the oil into a deep pot and heat to 375°F (190°C) over
moderate heat. Using a mandoline, cut the potato into wafer-
thin slices and plunge into cold water. When the oil has
reached the right temperature, drain the sliced potatoes and
put them on a clean dry cloth. Thoroughly dry the potatoes
before plunging a small amount at a time into the hot oil. Fry
them until golden brown, about 2 minutes. Remove immediately and place onto kitchen towel to absorb excess oil.
Sprinkle with salt and serve.

For the pizza dough

1 ½ tsp. •	7.5 mL	**dry yeast**
1 cup •	250 mL	**warm water**
pinch		**granulated sugar**
3 cups •	750 mL	**all-purpose flour**
¼ cup •	50 mL	**cornmeal**
1 Tbsp. •	15 mL	**chopped rosemary**
1 tsp. •	5 mL	**sea salt**
2 tsp. •	10 mL	**cracked black pepper**
¼ cup •	50 mL	**extra virgin olive oil**

Pizza of Asparagus, Morels
and Prosciutto

This recipe evolved from an experience I had on a working holiday to The Inn at Little Washington, in Virginia, USA. I was floored that such an outstanding restaurant was serving pizza, but when I saw it and tasted it, it was a revelation. I've tried to make it with other mushrooms and other cheeses, but it does not compare to this particular blend of ingredients.

This pizza dough recipe makes 12 pizza shells. Use 6 and freeze the other 6, tightly wrapped, for future use.

Combine the yeast with the warm water, sugar and ½ cup (125 mL) of the all-purpose flour. Let stand for 10 minutes. In the bowl of a food mixer fitted with a dough hook, combine the remaining ingredients. Add the yeast/flour mix to the ingredients in the bowl and mix on low speed to combine, 10 minutes. Put into a greased bowl, cover with plastic wrap and let rise until doubled.

Turn the dough out onto a lightly floured surface and punch down the dough. Divide into 6 small balls (each ball will weigh about 2 oz./60 g). Place the dough balls on a lightly floured baking tray and cover loosely with plastic wrap or kitchen towel. Leave in a warm place for the dough to rise again until doubled, about 30 minutes.

Preheat oven to 400°F (200°C).

Roll each ball as thin as possible with a rolling pin. Brush with water and bake until the dough is just set (no more than 5 minutes). Be careful not to let the dough get brown as this is just a base for the pizza.

MAKES 6 INDIVIDUAL PIZZAS

recipe continued on next page

Ingredients

2 Tbsp.	•	30 mL	**unsalted butter**
2 Tbsp.	•	30 mL	**olive oil**
1 lb.	•	500g	**fresh morel mushrooms**
1			**shallot, peeled and finely diced**
1 clove			**garlic, peeled and finely chopped**
$\frac{1}{2}$ cup	•	125 mL	**Sauvignon Blanc**
3 Tbsp.	•	45 mL	**35% cream**
2 Tbsp.	•	30 mL	**veal jus (page 243)**
2 tsp.	•	10 mL	**rosemary, chopped**
2 tsp.	•	10 mL	**thyme, chopped**
2 tsp.	•	10 mL	**Italian parsley, chopped**
			kosher salt and white pepper to taste
$\frac{1}{4}$ cup	•	50 mL	**unsalted butter, cubed**

morel mushroom paste

Set a large sauté pan over medium-high heat, then add the olive oil and butter. When the butter is frothy, add the mushrooms, shallot and garlic. Add the white wine and cream and bring to a boil. Reduce until only 2 Tbsp. (30 mL) of liquid remains. Add the veal glace and simmer until reduced by half. Add the herbs and stir to combine. Season with salt and pepper and remove from the heat.

Transfer half the contents of the pan to a food processor. Carefully add the cubed butter and process until smooth. Transfer to a bowl and refrigerate until needed. Reserve the rest of the mushrooms for the pizza topping.

Ingredients

½ cup	·	125 mL	**fontina cheese, grated**
½ cup	·	125 mL	**Asiago cheese, grated**
½ cup	·	125 mL	**Parmesan cheese, grated**
6			**pizza shells**
1 cup			**morel mushroom paste (page 58)**
			reserved morel mushrooms
36 spears			**asparagus, peeled and blanched**
6			**prosciutto slices, cut into thin julienne**
½ cup	·	125 mL	**extra virgin olive oil**
pinch			**fleur de sel**
6			**fresh basil leaves, torn into small pieces**

to assemble the pizzas

Combine the three cheeses and reserve. Lay the pizza shells on an ovenproof tray and divide the morel paste evenly among them. Using an offset spatula, spread the paste over the entire surface of each pizza shell leaving a 1-inch (2.5-cm) clear border around the outside of the paste.

Top each pizza with a generous sprinkling of the cheese mixture. Top each pizza with the reserved morels and the asparagus. Add some more cheese and bake for 20 minutes or until the cheese has melted and slightly browned. Remove the pizzas from the oven and sprinkle them with prosciutto. Drizzle with olive oil, sprinkle with fleur de sel and season with basil.

Serve immediately.

Ingredients

1 lb.	•	500 g	**fresh goat cheese**
2			**shallots, peeled and finely minced**
1 tsp.	•	5 mL	**fresh marjoram, finely chopped**
3 Tbsp.	•	45 mL	**fresh chives, finely minced**
½ cup	•	125 mL	**fresh tomato, peeled, seeded and diced**
½ cup	•	125 mL	**Sauvignon Blanc, reduced to 2 Tbsp. (30 mL)**
¼ cup	•	50 mL	**35% cream**
¼ cup	•	50 mL	**sour cream**
1			**lemon, juice only**
			kosher salt and white pepper to taste
2 cups	•	500 mL	**assorted dried fruit such as cherries, apples, apricots, blueberries, peaches and cranberries**

Goat Cheese and Sauvignon Blanc
Terrine with Dried Fruit

Goat cheese and Sauvignon Blanc are made for each other. Here, goat cheese is blended with the wine and fruit to create a memorable start to an elegant spring luncheon. If you do not have a terrine mold, you can make individual portions by packing the filling into a ramekin or even a plastic-lined coffee cup. Refrigerate so the filling can set, then enjoy.

In the bowl of a food mixer, combine all of the ingredients except the dried fruit and blend on medium speed until smooth. Fold in the dried fruit and blend to incorporate.

Line a 12-inch x 3-inch (30-cm x 8-cm) terrine mold (or loaf pan) with plastic wrap.

Spoon the goat cheese into the terrine mold and refrigerate for 3–4 hours.

Turn out the goat cheese terrine onto a cutting board and remove plastic.

Using a knife which has been warmed under a stream of hot water, cut into 1-inch (2.5-cm) slices. Place each slice onto a chilled plate and garnish with a selection of bread and flatbreads or crackers.

MAKES ONE 12-INCH /30-CM TERRINE

Lollipops

For these fun canapés, you will need to purchase lollipop sticks from a craft store. If you want to dress them up for a very special gathering, try wrapping each lollipop in cello plastic wrap and tying them individually with ribbon.

Shrimp Lollipops

Goat Cheese Lollipops

Smoked Salmon Lollipops

MAKES 12 OF EACH KIND OF LOLLIPOP
recipes continued on next pages

Ingredients

1 cup	• 250 mL	**raw shrimp, peeled and deveined**
1		**shallot, peeled and finely chopped**
1/2		**jalapeño pepper, seeded and finely minced**
1/2		**sweet pepper, seeded and finely chopped**
1 Tbsp.	• 15 mL	**cilantro, finely chopped**
pinch		**cayenne pepper**
1 Tbsp.	• 15 mL	**sesame seeds, lightly toasted**
2 cups	• 500 mL	**vegetable oil for deep frying**
1/2 cup	• 125 mL	**all-purpose flour**
2		**eggs, slightly beaten**
1 cup	• 250 mL	**bread crumbs**
		kosher salt and white pepper to taste

Shrimp Lollipops

Purée the shrimp in a food processor until smooth. Transfer the shrimp purée to a stainless steel bowl. Add the shallot, jalapeño, sweet pepper, cilantro, cayenne and sesame seeds and combine thoroughly. Refrigerate for 3 hours.

Remove the shrimp purée from the fridge and, using your hands, form 12 balls (each ball of shrimp mix should be the circumference of a nickel). Insert an 8-inch (20-cm) wooden skewer into each shrimp ball. Refrigerate.

Heat the deep frying oil to 360°F (185°C).

Take the shrimp lollipops from the fridge and dip each one first into the flour, then the egg and finally the bread crumbs. Make sure the shrimp lollipops are well coated with the bread crumbs. Carefully lower each shrimp lollipop into the hot oil and cook until golden brown.

Ingredients

$\frac{1}{2}$ cup	· 125 mL	**35% cream**
$\frac{1}{4}$ cup	· 50 mL	**dry white wine**
1		**shallot, peeled and finely chopped**
1 tsp.	· 5 mL	**thyme, finely chopped**
$\frac{1}{2}$ lb.	· 250 g	**goat cheese**

Goat Cheese Lollipops

In a small saucepan bring the cream, wine and shallot to a boil. Reduce the heat and simmer until reduced by half. Transfer to a bowl and add the thyme and goat cheese. Using a wooden spoon, combine thoroughly. Refrigerate for 1 hour.

Divide the mixture into 12 equally sized balls (using a scale will make this easier). Using your hands, form the 12 balls into lollipop shapes (each ball should be the circumference of a nickel). Refrigerate.

Ingredients

$\frac{1}{4}$ cup	· 50 mL	**sesame seeds, lightly toasted**
$\frac{1}{4}$ cup	· 50 mL	**sweet paprika**
$\frac{1}{4}$ cup	· 50 mL	**hazelnuts, toasted and ground**
$\frac{1}{4}$ cup	· 50 mL	**poppy seeds**

to finish the Goat Cheese Lollipops

Place each ingredient in a separate bowl. Roll an equal number of goat cheese lollipops in each of the coatings, insert lollipop sticks in the balls and refrigerate until ready to serve.

Ingredients

$1/2$ cup •	125 mL	**Smoked Salmon Cream (page 67)**
$1/2$ cup •	125 mL	**cream cheese**
$1/2$ cup •	125 mL	**smoked salmon, finely chopped or puréed in a food processor**
1		**shallot, peeled and finely chopped**
1		**lemon, zest and juice of**
pinch		**cayenne pepper**

Smoked Salmon Lollipops

Combine all the ingredients in a bowl and mix until well blended. Refrigerate for 1–2 hours. Divide the smoked salmon lollipop mixture into 12 equal portions and then using your hands, form 12 balls (each ball should be the circumference of a nickel). Carefully insert a lollipop stick into each ball and serve.

Ingredients

2 Tbsp. ·	30 mL	**olive oil**
2 Tbsp. ·	30 mL	**butter**
½		**onion, peeled and finely chopped**
½		**carrot, peeled and finely chopped**
1 clove		**garlic, peeled and minced**
1 cup ·	250 mL	**smoked salmon, chopped**
1 cup ·	250 mL	**white wine**
1 cup ·	250 mL	**35% cream**
2 tsp. ·	10 mL	**tomato paste**
1 Tbsp. ·	15 mL	**champagne vinegar**
1 Tbsp. ·	15 mL	**dill, chopped**
		kosher salt and white pepper to taste

Smoked Salmon Cream

In a medium saucepot, melt the butter and olive oil over medium heat. Add the onion, carrot and garlic and continue cooking for 10 minutes, stirring frequently. Add the smoked salmon and allow it to cook until it changes color and easily flakes, about 8 minutes. Add the white wine, cream and tomato paste. Simmer until slightly reduced.

Pass the sauce through a fine sieve and return it to a gentle simmer. Reduce the sauce until it coats a spoon. Pass the sauce through a fine mesh sieve and discard the solids. Reserve the sauce in a bowl and add the vinegar and dill. Season with salt and pepper to taste. Transfer sauce to a bowl and refrigerate until needed.

HOW TO PICK, SHELL AND BLANCH FRESH FAVA BEANS

One of my favorite tasks during the summer is to pick fava beans. I love the look of them, the smell and the entire almost ritualistic technique required to make them edible. First of all, make yourself a nice big pot of tea and find a comfortable chair to sit in (this will take a while).

Second, put on your favorite cooking music (perhaps the soundtrack of *Big Night*?) Now you're ready. Working with one pod at a time, rip off the end and run your thumb down through the entire bean. As your thumb bumps into a fava bean flick it out of the pod and into a container. Repeat this process until you have the required amount for the recipe.

Next, set a large pot of water on the stove and bring it to a rapid boil. Add some salt (a generous pinch or two). Prepare an ice bath. Quickly submerge the fava beans into the boiling water. Count to ten (one steamboat, two steamboat, three steamboat, etc.). Quickly remove the beans from the water and submerge them in an ice bath. When all the beans are chilled in the ice bath drain them and place them in a bowl.

Next, using your thumb and index finger, pinch off the skins of the fava bean to reveal the sweet bean inside. When all the beans have been peeled, continue with the recipe.

Tomatoes Stuffed with Fava Beans
and Goat Cheese

This dish, served either as an appetizer or as an accompaniment to extremely fresh, lightly grilled fish is the epitome of what a Sauvignon Blanc dish should be. It is fresh, colorful and tasty. It's also easy to prepare at the last moment once a few simple preparations are completed. Shelling, blanching and peeling fava beans requires some work, but can be quite therapeutic!

Ingredients

1/4 cup	•	50 mL	**white wine vinegar**
3/4 cup	•	175 ml	**olive oil**
1/2 cup	•	125 mL	**fresh tomato, seeded and diced**
1 cup	•	250 mL	**fava beans, shelled, blanched and peeled**
			kosher salt and white pepper to taste
2 Tbsp.	•	30 mL	**parsley, chopped**
6			**large, ripe beefsteak tomatoes, blanched, with insides scooped out**
1/2 cup	•	125 mL	**goat cheese, crumbled**

Combine the vinegar and olive oil and whisk until well blended. Mix in the diced tomato and the fava beans. Season with salt and pepper. Stir in the parsley.

Divide the fava bean mix among the hollowed-out beefsteak tomatoes. Top each tomato with goat cheese and serve.

MAKES 6 SERVINGS

Poached Pickerel
with Watercress Sauce

This refreshingly light dish is perfect in the spring when the watercress is fragrant and the pickerel is ultra fresh. It makes a satisfying entrée for lunch or an elegant appetizer. Leave the skin on the pickerel fillets and, using a small sharp knife, score the skin to get the most benefit from the poaching technique.

Ingredients

2 lbs. · 1 kg		**pickerel fillets, divided into 6 portions**
		kosher salt and white pepper to taste
2 lbs. · 1 kg		**picked watercress, stems discarded, blanched**
3 Tbsp. · 45 mL		**unsalted butter, at room temperature**
½ cup · 125 mL		**onion, peeled and finely chopped**
½ cup · 125 mL		**carrot, peeled and finely chopped**
1 cup · 250 mL		**Fish Stock (page 50)**
½ cup · 125 mL		**white wine**
3 sprigs		**dill, chopped**
3 sprigs		**Italian parsley, chopped**
½ cup · 125 mL		**35% cream**
1		**lemon, juice of**

Season the pickerel with salt and pepper to taste.

Purée the blanched watercress leaves in a food processor until smooth. Reserve.

Spread the butter over the bottom of a pan that has an ovenproof handle and is large enough to hold all the fish. Add the onion and carrot, making a bed for the fish. Place the fish on the vegetables with the skin side up. Add the fish stock and white wine and sprinkle with the herbs.

Preheat oven to 350°F (180°C).

Place the fish on the vegetables with the skin side up. Add the fish stock and white wine and sprinkle with the herbs.

Place the pan with the fish over medium-high heat and heat the liquid to a gentle simmer. Transfer into the oven to finish poaching, about 6–8 minutes. Remove from the pan and, using a slotted spatula, gently lift the pickerel out of the poaching liquid. Keep warm.

Bring the cooking liquid to a boil then reduce by one-third. Add the cream and return to a boil. Reduce the sauce until it coats the back of a spoon. Add the reserved watercress purée, lemon juice and salt and pepper. Spoon the sauce over the fish and serve.

MAKES 6 SERVINGS

Ingredients

4		**small leeks (white part only), washed and patted dry**
18		**sea scallops**
30 spears		**asparagus, blanched**
$^1/_4$ cup	• 50 mL	**olive oil**
		kosher salt and white pepper to taste
3 cups	• 750 mL	**baby salad greens**

Asparagus Scallop Salad
with Sweet and Sour Dressing

This recipe is meant to celebrate the official opening of the barbecue season. It should be served as an appetizer or a light meal to be enjoyed outdoors.

Preheat grill to high.

Cut each leek in half lengthwise and place in a bowl. Place the scallops and asparagus in separate bowls. Season the leeks, scallops and asparagus with an equal amount of olive oil and salt and pepper.

Grill the leeks until they are charred around the edges. Remove from the grill and, when they are cool to the touch, cut them into 1-inch (2.5-cm) slices. Keep warm.

Add the scallops to the grill and grill for 2 minutes on each side. Remove from the heat and keep them warm.

Place the asparagus on the grill and grill until nicely charred and cooked through. Remove from the heat and keep warm.

MAKES 6 SERVINGS

recipe continued on next page

Ingredients

1		**shallot, peeled and finely minced**
1		**garlic clove, peeled and finely minced**
½ tsp.	· 2 mL	**Dijon mustard**
		kosher salt and white pepper to taste
½ cup	· 125 mL	**olive oil**
¼ cup	· 50 mL	**champagne vinegar**
¼ cup	· 50 mL	**white wine**
1		**lemon, juice of**

Sweet and Sour Dressing

Combine the shallot, garlic and mustard with salt and pepper, olive oil, vinegar and white wine. Whisk until well blended and reserve.

Divide the leeks among 6 large dinner plates, placing them in the center of the plate. Top the leeks with the asparagus and top the asparagus with the baby greens. Place the scallops around the plate and add a generous drizzle of dressing.

Ingredients

2 Tbsp.	· 30 mL	**olive oil**
2 Tbsp.	· 30 mL	**unsalted butter**
1 cup	· 250 mL	**onion, peeled and finely chopped**
1 cup	· 250 mL	**carrot, peeled and chopped**
2		**leeks (white part only), chopped**
2 cups	· 500 mL	**artichokes, cubed**
2 cloves		**garlic, peeled and minced**
2 Tbsp.	· 30 mL	**black olives, pits removed**
¼ cup	· 50 mL	**Sauvignon Blanc**
½ cup	· 125 mL	**brandy**
3 cups	· 750 mL	**Chicken Stock (page 267) or water**
2 Tbsp.	· 30 mL	**lemon juice**
2 Tbsp.	· 30 mL	**anchovy paste**
dash		**hot pepper sauce**
1 cup	· 250 mL	**sour cream**
1 Tbsp.	· 15 mL	**rosemary, chopped**
		kosher salt and white pepper to taste

Artichoke Tapenade

Artichokes contain an acid called cynarin that can make wine taste sweeter than it is. To counter the effect of cynarin, use acidic ingredients such as lemon juice, anchovies and wine, which will balance nicely with the rather forward taste of the artichokes.

In a large stockpot, heat the oil and add the butter. When the butter is frothy, add the onion, carrot, leeks and artichoke and cook for 10 minutes, stirring frequently.

Add the garlic, stir frequently for 5 minutes, then add the olives. Add the white wine, brandy and chicken stock or water. Bring to a rapid boil. Reduce heat and simmer for 35 to 45 minutes or until the vegetables are cooked through.

Transfer to a food processor and purée until smooth. Blend in the lemon juice, anchovy paste and hot sauce. Refrigerate the tapenade until it is completely cool. Stir in the sour cream and the rosemary and adjust seasonings. Serve with assorted breads.

MAKES 4 CUPS/1 L

Spiked Gazpacho

This is a wine country version of the classic refreshing soup from Mexico. My version is based on a "stock" made from cucumber, tomato juice, Sauvignon Blanc and fresh coriander. The vegetables are interchangeable and making substitutions won't jeopardize the refreshing experience of drinking this soup during the hot summer months. Try serving in oversized martini glasses for dramatic effect.

Ingredients

2		cucumbers, peeled and chopped
2 cups	500 mL	tomato juice
1 cup	250 mL	Sauvignon Blanc
2 cups	500 mL	sparkling mineral water
3 Tbsp.	45 mL	coriander, finely chopped
2		lemons, juice of
		kosher salt and white pepper to taste
1		zucchini, finely diced and blanched
1		yellow squash, finely diced and blanched
1		red onion, finely diced
2		tomatoes, seeded and finely diced
1		avocado, peeled and finely diced
1		red pepper, seeded and finely chopped
1		yellow pepper, seeded and finely chopped
1		jalapeño chili, seeded and finely chopped
2 Tbsp.	30 mL	thyme, finely chopped
3 Tbsp.	45 mL	chervil, finely chopped

In a food processor, purée the cucumber with the tomato juice, Sauvignon Blanc, mineral water and coriander. Season the purée with the lemon juice, salt and pepper. Pass the liquid through a fine mesh sieve. Discard the solids and refrigerate the liquid.

In a large bowl combine the remaining ingredients. Combine the vegetables with the chilled liquid. Refrigerate overnight. Season with salt and pepper.

Spoon the soup into 6 chilled bowls and serve.

MAKES 6 SERVINGS

Ingredients

2 Tbsp.	•	30 mL	**olive oil**
2 Tbsp.	•	30 mL	**butter**
1			**onion, peeled and chopped**
2 cloves			**garlic, peeled and finely chopped**
1 Tbsp.	•	15 mL	**fresh ginger, peeled and chopped**
3 cups	•	750 mL	**carrots, peeled and chopped**
2 cups	•	500 mL	**Sauvignon Blanc**
3 cups	•	750 mL	**Vegetable Mushroom Stock (page 43)**
3			**apples, peeled, cored and cubed**
$\frac{1}{2}$ cup	•	125 mL	**unpasteurized apple cider**
1 tsp.	•	5 mL	**sage, finely chopped**
			kosher salt and white pepper to taste
pinch			**fresh ground nutmeg (to taste)**
$\frac{1}{2}$ cup	•	125 mL	**crème fraîche (page 79)**

Gingered Carrot and Apple Soup

For some happy reason, the flavor of ginger is particularly suited to Sauvignon Blanc. Perhaps the exotic gooseberry and lychee nut flavors of the wine match nicely with the peppery sweetness of ginger. In this recipe, the wine and the ginger combine to highlight the refreshing flavor of carrots. This soup can be enjoyed hot with a dollop of sour cream or chilled in a tumbler. Either way, it's a taste sensation.

Heat a large soup pot over moderately high heat and add the olive oil and butter. When the butter becomes frothy, add the onion. Stir frequently until the onion is soft and translucent, about 5 minutes, then add the garlic and ginger. Continue stirring until the garlic and ginger have released their aromas, about 10 minutes.

Add the carrots, wine and vegetable stock. Bring the soup to a boil, reduce the heat to a simmer and cook for 15 minutes. Add the apples and the apple cider and cook for another 10 minutes. The carrots and apples must be cooked all the way through.

Pour the soup through a strainer to separate the solids from the liquid. Keep the liquid warm. Transfer the solids to a food processor or a blender and process until very smooth. Using a ladle add in the liquid to the purée until you have the consistency you desire.

When you have achieved the desired consistency, return the soup to a boil. Turn off the heat and stir in the sage, salt and pepper. Pour into warmed soup bowls and serve with a dollop of crème fraîche.

MAKES 6 SERVINGS

Crème Fraîche

This mild, slightly sour cream is to the French what sour cream is to North Americans. A dollop of crème fraîche makes an important contribution to soups, sauces and other recipes.

Ingredients

1 cup	• 250 mL	**35% cream**
3 Tbsp.	• 45 mL	**full fat buttermilk**

Whisk to combine the cream and buttermilk. Transfer to a bowl or mason jar and cover with plastic wrap. Let stand in a warm place until the cream thickens, usually within 24 hours. When it is thick, it will keep for a week in the refrigerator.

Ingredients

3		whole beets, washed, unpeeled
6 cups · 1.5 L		cold water
1 cup · 250 mL		fresh goat cheese, at room temperature

Harvest Beets and Goat Cheese
with Pumpkin Sauvignon Blanc Vinaigrette

This recipe is an homage to the wonderful flavors of beets and goat cheese. These two flavors were meant for each other. Combined with the subtle nuttiness of toasted pumpkin seeds and the generous acidity of the Sauvignon Blanc, this is sure to be an autumn classic.

In a large pot, cover the beets with the cold water and place over medium heat. Simmer the beets until soft (45 minutes). Drain the beets and rinse under cold running water. Using your fingers, rub the skin away from the beets until they are completely cleaned. Transfer the beets to kitchen towel to pat dry.

Cut the beets into $\frac{1}{2}$-inch (1-cm) slices. Divide the beets among 6 dinner plates. Crumble goat cheese over the beets. Drizzle with the vinaigrette. Serve immediately.

MAKES 6 SERVINGS

Pumpkin Sauvignon Blanc Vinaigrette

Ingredients

$\frac{1}{2}$ cup · 125 mL		Sauvignon Blanc
2		shallots, peeled and finely chopped
2 tsp. · 10 mL		Dijon mustard
$\frac{1}{4}$ cup · 50 mL		pumpkin seed oil
$\frac{1}{2}$ cup · 125 mL		olive oil
$\frac{1}{4}$ cup · 50 mL		sherry wine vinegar
1		lemon, juice of
$\frac{1}{4}$ cup · 50 mL		toasted pumpkin seeds

Place the Sauvignon Blanc in a small saucepot set over medium heat and simmer until only 2 Tbsp. (30 mL) of wine remains. Remove from the heat and let cool to room temperature.

Combine the shallots, mustard, pumpkin seed oil, olive oil, sherry wine vinegar, reserved reduced wine and lemon juice in a bowl and and whisk just until emulsified. Add the toasted pumpkin seeds and reserve.

Ingredients

1½ cups •	375 mL	**grated carrot**
1 cup •	250 mL	**grated celery**
1 cup •	250 mL	**grated onion**
½ cup •	125 mL	**grated red pepper**
½ cup •	125 mL	**grated green pepper**
¾ cup •	175 mL	**ground walnuts**
1 cup •	250 mL	**scallions, finely chopped**
2		**eggs**
		hot pepper sauce to taste
		sesame oil to taste
		kosher salt and white pepper to taste
1 cup •	250 mL	**ground crackers or bread crumbs**
2 Tbsp. •	30 mL	**unsalted butter**
2 Tbsp. •	30 mL	**olive oil**

Vegetable Burgers

This recipe will delight the vegetarians in your crowd. It is easy to prepare and many carnivores like it too. I created this for the 1997 Vineyard Jazz festival. It was such a hit that I have featured it on many autumn menus and it continues to draw rave reviews.

Mix together the carrots, celery, onion and peppers and leave in a colander to drain for 1 hour. Press out as much liquid as possible and transfer the vegetables to a large bowl.

Preheat oven to 400°F (200°C).

Add the walnuts, scallions, eggs, hot sauce, sesame oil and seasonings. Add the cracker or bread crumbs and mix well to form a firm mixture. Form into patties.

Melt the butter and olive oil in an ovenproof pan over medium heat, Place the patties in the pan and bake for 10 minutes on each side or until golden brown. Serve.

MAKES 6 BURGERS

Ingredients

2 Tbsp.	• 30 mL	**olive oil**
2 Tbsp.	• 30 mL	**unsalted butter**
$^{1}/_{2}$ cup	• 125 mL	**onions, peeled and chopped**
1 clove		**clove garlic, peeled and chopped**
1		**leek (white part only), chopped**
3 cups	• 750 mL	**Jerusalem artichoke, peeled and chopped**
1 cup	• 250 mL	**potato, peeled and chopped**
6 cups	• 1.5 L	**Mushroom Vegetable Stock (page 43)**
2 Tbsp.	• 30 mL	**unsalted butter**
		kosher salt and white pepper to taste

Jerusalem Artichoke Soup

One of the most underused winter vegetables is the Jerusalem artichoke. It is not really an artichoke at all, but is a variety of sunflower. Its name is derived from the Italian word for sunflower which is "girasole."

In a large soup pot, melt the olive oil and 2 Tbsp. (30 mL) butter over moderately high heat.

Add the onion, garlic and leek. Sauté until the onion and leek are soft but not brown, stirring frequently. Add the artichoke, potato and stock. Bring to a boil, then reduce to a simmer until the potato is cooked, about 20 minutes.

Transfer the soup to a blender and purée until smooth. Return the soup to the pot and bring to a boil. Add the remaining 2 Tbsp. (30 mL) butter and season with salt and pepper. When the butter has melted, stir the soup and serve.

MAKES 6 SERVINGS

Ingredients

¹⁄₂ cup •	125 mL	**olive oil**
1		**onion, peeled and finely chopped**
1 clove		**garlic, peeled and finely chopped**
1 lb. •	500 g	**chicken livers, cleaned**
		kosher salt and white pepper to taste
¹⁄₂ cup •	125 mL	**brandy**
¹⁄₂ cup •	125 mL	**cold butter, cubed**
¹⁄₄ cup •	50 mL	**green zucchini, finely diced**
¹⁄₄ cup •	50 mL	**yellow zucchini, finely diced**
¹⁄₄ cup •	50 mL	**peeled carrot, finely diced**
¹⁄₄ cup •	50 mL	**red onion, finely diced**
¹⁄₄ cup •	50 mL	**red pepper, finely diced**
2 tsp. •	10 mL	**sage, chopped**
2 tsp. •	10 mL	**thyme, chopped**
2 tsp. •	10 mL	**rosemary, chopped**

Chicken Liver Vegetable Pâté
with Quince Marmalade

I prepared this for my buddies during a Super Bowl party a few years ago and it was a huge favorite. It's a great dish to prepare for "pot luck" for an informal gathering. Serve it with some great crusty bread, vegetable sticks or crackers.

In a large sauté pan, heat ¹⁄₄ cup (50 mL) of the olive oil and add the onion and garlic. Reduce the heat to low and stir frequently until the onion is caramelized, about 15 minutes. Add the chicken livers and cook through until no pink is showing. Season with salt and pepper. Add the brandy and carefully set alight. When the flame subsides, pour the contents of the pan into a food processor and, with the motor running, add the butter. Purée until smooth. Pour the chicken liver pâté into a bowl and reserve in the refrigerator until well chilled, about 3 hours.

Meanwhile, in another hot pan, heat the remaining olive oil. Add the vegetables and stir frequently for 10 minutes until the vegetables are softened, but not browned. Transfer the sautéed vegetables onto some kitchen towel to absorb excess grease. Place the vegetables in a bowl and refrigerate until well chilled. Using a rubber spatula, pour the vegetables out of the bowl and over the chicken liver pâté. Sprinkle with the chopped herbs and refrigerate until ready to serve.

MAKES 8–12 SERVINGS

recipe continued on next page

Quince Marmalade

One of my favorite fall and winter fruits is the quince. Quince have an appearance which may resemble pears and apples but the perfume from a quince in incomparable. Quince must be cooked to fully enjoy their remarkable flavour. They can be baked, poached, sauté and in any case you must peel them first and submerge them in acidulated water to keep them from turning brown. This recipe is ideal for pâtés but can also be used as a condiment to crusty bread.

Ingredients

3 lbs.	•	$1\frac{1}{2}$ kg	quince
$\frac{1}{2}$ cup	•	125 mL	lemon juice
2			lemons, halved, zest reserved, cut into $\frac{1}{8}$ths
2 Tbsp.	•	30 mL	fresh ginger, peeled and finely chopped
3 cups	•	750 mL	granulated sugar
2 Tbsp.	•	30 mL	unsalted butter
1			onion, peeled and finely diced
1 Tbsp.	•	15 mL	fresh ginger, peeled and finely chopped
1 tsp.	•	5 mL	ground cumin
$\frac{1}{2}$ tsp.	•	$2\frac{1}{2}$ mL	mustard seeds
2 cups	•	500 mL	cooked quince
$\frac{1}{2}$ cup	•	125 mL	quince syrup (liquid the quince were cooled in)

Cut each quince into quarters, then peel and core them with a small utility knife. Reserve the peel and cores. Submerge the cleaned quince in the lemon juice and enough water to cover them.

Place the peel and cores in a small pot and cover with cold water. Place the pot on medium-high heat and simmer for 35 minutes. Strain the liquid into another pot and discard the peels and cores. Reduce the liquid by half and reserve.

Strain the reserved quince through a colander and place in a pot. Add just enough cold water to cover and add the lemons. Add the ginger and sugar and bring to a simmer over medium heat. Add the reduced quince liquid from the peel and cores. Continue to simmer for 35 minutes or until the quince have softened. Remove from the heat and let cool in the cooking liquid at room temperature.

In a medium sauté pan set over medium heat, add the butter. When the butter is frothy, add in the onion and ginger. Cook, stirring frequently, until the onion is translucent and the ginger is fragrant. Add the cumin and mustard seed. Stir frequently and add the cooked quince and quince syrup. Bring to a simmer and cook for 10 minutes. Remove from the heat and transfer to a bowl. Refrigerate the marmalade until set then serve with the chicken liver vegetable pâté.

MAKES 8 CUPS (2 LITRES)

Ingredients

6 cups	·	1.5 L	**vegetable oil**
6 florets			**broccoli, blanched**
6 florets			**cauliflower, blanched**
4			**oyster mushrooms**
6 spears			**asparagus**
6			**baby carrots, peeled and blanched**
6 leaves			**baby spinach**
1 cup	·	250 mL	**tempura batter (page 88)**
2 Tbsp.	·	30 mL	**olive oil**
3 lbs.	·	1.5 kg	**sea scallops**
			kosher salt and white pepper to taste
$\frac{1}{2}$ cup	·	125 mL	**Curried Parsnips (page 88)**
$\frac{1}{4}$ cup	·	50 mL	**ginger carrot juice reduction (page 89)**

Atlantic Sea Scallops
with Vegetable Tempura

Coating fresh vegetables in a light and fluffy tempura batter is a delicious way to enjoy the season's bounty. This recipe combines the gentle sweetness of fresh scallops with a lightly curried parsnip sauce and tempura vegetables.

Using a large pot heat the vegetable oil to 375°F (190°C).

Dip the vegetables into the tempura batter one at a time and deep fry until they have browned slightly, about 3 minutes. Using a slotted spoon remove the vegetables onto a paper towel to catch excess oil. Keep the vegetables warm. Keep the oil at a constant temperature.

In a sauté pan, heat 1 Tbsp. (15 mL) of olive oil over medium-high heat. Season the scallops with salt and pepper to taste and cook until golden brown, 4 minutes per side. Remove from the heat and keep warm.

Plunge the deep-fried vegetables back into the hot oil for 30 seconds. Remove from the oil and keep warm.

In two small saucepots, heat the curried parsnip and the reduced ginger carrot reduction. Divide the parsnip, scallops and tempura vegetables among 6 dinner plates. Spoon over the ginger carrot juice reduction and serve.

MAKES 6 SERVINGS

recipe continued on next page

Ingredients

³/₄ cup	• 175 mL	**cornstarch**
3 cups	• 750 mL	**cake flour**
2 tsp.	• 10 mL	**baking powder**
1 tsp.	• 5 mL	**kosher salt**
6 cups	• 1.5 L	**sparkling mineral water**

for the tempura batter

Combine the dry ingredients in a bowl and stir to mix thoroughly. To make the batter, measure out 2 parts of sparkling mineral water and 1 part of the dry ingredients and whisk to combine until very smooth. Let sit for 15 minutes before using.

Ingredients

1 Tbsp.	• 15 mL	**olive oil**
1 Tbsp.	• 15 mL	**unsalted butter**
1		**onion, peeled and chopped**
2 cloves		**garlic, peeled and chopped**
2 tsp.	• 10 mL	**mild curry powder**
1 tsp.	• 5 mL	**ground cumin**
1 tsp.	• 5 mL	**ground coriander seed**
4		**large parsnips, peeled and chopped**
1 cup	• 250 mL	**Fish Stock (page 50)**
1 tsp.	• 5 mL	**chopped fresh cilantro**
		kosher salt and white pepper to taste

Curried Parsnips

In a medium saucepan, heat the oil and butter over medium heat. When the butter is frothy, add the onion, garlic, curry powder, cumin and coriander. Cook until the onion is translucent, about 4 minutes, stirring regularly to prevent the onion from browning. Add the parsnips and the fish stock. Bring to a boil, then reduce to a simmer. Cook for 20 minutes, or until the parsnips are cooked through and little liquid remains.

Transfer to a food processor and purée until smooth. Add the chopped cilantro and season with salt and pepper. Keep warm until ready to serve.

Ingredients

2 cups	•	500 mL	**carrot juice**
1 Tbsp.	•	15 mL	**unsalted butter**
1 Tbsp.	•	15 mL	**fresh ginger, peeled and chopped**
1			**shallot, peeled and finely diced**
2 tsp.	•	10 mL	**mustard seeds**
1 cup	•	250 mL	**late harvest Vidal**
¼ cup	•	50 mL	**unsalted butter, cubed**
			kosher salt and white pepper to taste

for the ginger carrot juice reduction

Pour the carrot juice into a saucepan over high heat and bring
to a boil. In a separate saucepan, over medium heat, melt 1 Tbsp.
(15 mL) of butter and add the ginger and shallot. Stir for 4
minutes or until the shallot is translucent. Add the mustard
seeds and late harvest Vidal. Reduce until the Vidal has thickened to syrup. Add the hot carrot juice to the reduced Vidal
and continue to boil until only 4 Tbsp. (60 mL) of gingered
carrot juice reduction remains. Season with salt and pepper.
Keep warm.

Chicken Legs Marinated
in Yogurt and Lime

The combination of yogurt and lime is refreshing and tasty. Combining them in a marinade with spices is an exciting way to take common chicken legs to a different level. The acidity of yogurt and lime makes the meat tender and extremely flavorful.

Ingredients

2 Tbsp. • 30 mL		**unsalted butter**
2		**shallots, peeled and finely diced**
1 Tbsp. • 15 mL		**fresh ginger, peeled and finely diced**
1 tsp. • 5 mL		**ground cumin**
1 tsp. • 5 mL		**ground allspice**
½ cup • 125 mL		**Sauvignon Blanc**
4		**limes, juice and zest of**
2 cups • 500 mL		**yogurt**
6		**chicken legs**
		kosher salt and white pepper to taste

Melt the butter in a small saucepan and add the shallots and ginger. Cook for 5 minutes, stirring frequently over medium heat. Add the cumin, allspice, wine and lime juice. Increase the heat to high and reduce the liquid by half.

Strain the liquid through a fine sieve. Discard the solids. Refrigerate the strained liquid.

Combine the cooled liquid with the yogurt. Sprinkle with the lime zest and stir to combine.

Season the chicken with salt and pepper and place in a casserole. Make sure the chicken fits snugly. Pour the yogurt over the chicken legs, making sure to cover the entire chicken. Refrigerate overnight.

Preheat oven to 375°F (190°C).

Remove the chicken from the marinade and place in an oven-proof dish. Bake the chicken until it is cooked through and the juices run clear, about 45 minutes. Serve immediately.

MAKES 6 SERVINGS

Spring

Canadian Crab Cakes

Smoked Salmon, Lobster
  and Crab Terrine

Pickerel
  with Tomato Confit
  and Riesling Reduction

Chicken
  with Four Peppercorn Crust

Summer

Sweet Pepper Bisque

Pork Tenderloin
  with Niagara Succotash

Pickerel
  with Cucumber Noodles
  and Tomato Butter

Ling Cod
  with Oyster Mushroom Sauce
  and Mashed Potatoes

A Lobster Tasting Menu

Riesling

AS WINEMAKER J.L. GROUX IS FOND OF SAYING, "GOOD WINE is made in the vineyard." The ability of a vine to produce grapes that are then made into great wine is best exemplified by the great German varietal known as Riesling. This classic German grape is notable for being able to represent the individual nuances of the terroir while maintaining its distinctive varietal character. A thick-skinned grape, it shows a remarkable resistance to cold weather and, because of its long ripening cycle, it is able to extract more nutrients out of the earth than any other variety of grape.

Riesling is one of the world's most frequently planted varietals. From light, floral and elegant to big and full-

Autumn

Salsify Soup
with Pan-Seared Scallops

Skate
with Caper Brown Butter Sauce

Smoked Pork Loin
with Riesling Creamed Corn and Fritters

Saffron Salmon
with Pine Nut Apple Salad

Winter

Pear and Parsnip Soup

Roasted Halibut
with Sweet Potato Purée
and Pickled Onions

Smoked Chicken Pasta
with Walnuts, Endive and Parsley

Veal Baked with 40 Cloves of Garlic

bodied, I believe that the general wine-drinking population has not yet caught on to the full beauty of this grape. It is still in the shadow of the Chardonnay. However, it is starting to catch on. Sommeliers, ones who know and appreciate the intricacies of this variety, are starting to recommend it and people are responding favorably.

Riesling wine is a great food-matching wine. Its varied styles can accommodate rich or light-textured foods—from pork, veal, smoked meats and chicken to almost any fish and shellfish (as you will notice in the Riesling menu); from a variety of cheeses to eggs and pasta dishes. Riesling can match an enormous range and depth of flavors. Older Rieslings with complex aromas of almonds, honey, minerals and petrol are perfectly suited to rich and festive dishes. Younger wines with their peach, apricot and honeysuckle fruit and acidity are perfect for mildly spiced appetizers and hors d'oeuvres.

Riesling's unique characteristics are particularity well suited to contrast and enhance the repertoire of my wine country cuisine.

Ingredients

1 cup	•	250 mL	**all-purpose flour**
1 tsp.	•	5 mL	**curry powder**
1 tsp.	•	5 mL	**ground cumin**
1 tsp.	•	5 mL	**ground ginger**
1 tsp.	•	5 mL	**cayenne pepper**
2 Tbsp.	•	30 mL	**kosher salt**
1 lb.	•	500 g	**crabmeat**
2			**eggs**
¼ cup	•	50 mL	**red pepper, diced**
½ cup	•	125 mL	**green onion, finely chopped**
¼ cup	•	50 mL	**mayonnaise (page 13)**
1 Tbsp.	•	15 mL	**Dijon mustard**
			kosher salt and white pepper to taste
2 Tbsp.	•	30 mL	**vegetable oil**
2 Tbsp.	•	30 mL	**unsalted butter**

Canadian Crab Cakes

My wife is from the Canadian Maritimes, and when we visit I crave the delicately sweet taste of crab. The best crab cakes use very little filler and are loose and flaky. A dense crab cake probably contains plenty of bread crumbs or flour. This recipe uses very little flour for a delicious true crab flavor. I also like to include a little subtle spice in my crab cakes to help lift the flavor.

In a mixing bowl, combine the flour with the curry powder, cumin, ginger, cayenne pepper and salt, then mix thoroughly and reserve.

Combine the crabmeat, eggs, pepper, onion, mayonnaise, mustard and salt and pepper to taste. Refrigerate the mixture for 30 minutes. Form the crab cakes into 3-inch (8-cm) disks (you may wish to make them smaller or larger), and reserve.

Preheat a large sauté pan over moderately high heat. Add the oil and butter and heat until the butter is frothy. Dip each crab cake first in the seasoned flour to coat completely then immediately into the sauté pan. Repeat. Cook the crab cakes for 1 to 2 minutes on each side, or until golden brown. Serve warm.

MAKES 24 CRAB CAKES

Ingredients

2 lbs.	·	1 kg	**smoked salmon, sliced thin**
1/2 lb.	·	250 g	**crabmeat**
1/2 lb.	·	250 g	**lobster meat cut into 1-inch (2.5-cm) pieces**
1/2 lb.	·	250 g	**cream cheese**
1/2 cup	·	125 mL	**red pepper, finely diced**
1/2 cup	·	125 mL	**yellow pepper, finely diced**
1/2 cup	·	125 mL	**green zucchini, finely diced**
1/2 cup	·	125 mL	**green onions, finely diced**
3			**lemons, juice and zest of**
2 Tbsp.	·	30 mL	**tarragon, chopped**
2 Tbsp.	·	30 mL	**dill, chopped**
2 Tbsp.	·	30 mL	**chives, chopped**
24 sheets			**gelatin**
2 cups	·	500 mL	**warm water**
			kosher salt and white pepper to taste

Smoked Salmon, Lobster
and Crab Terrine

The refined and delicate taste of this terrine is a great way to start the spring season. The smokiness of the salmon is a perfect foil for the sweetness of the crab and lobster. Serve this terrine cold for an elegant dinner. It matches well with a crisp and refined Riesling.

Line a terrine mold measuring approximately 12 inches long, 3 inches wide and 3 inches deep (30 cm x 8 cm x 8 cm) with plastic wrap. Cover the bottom and sides of the mold with slightly overlapping slices of smoked salmon. In the bowl of an electric mixer mix the crabmeat, lobster and cream cheese on low speed until thoroughly combined.

Combine the peppers, zucchini, green onions, lemon zest, tarragon, dill and chives and reserve.

Melt the gelatin in the warm water, stir to dissolve, let cool to room temperature then add to the crab/cream cheese mix. Fold in the vegetables and herbs and combine thoroughly. Season with salt and pepper and the lemon juice.

Pour the mixture into the smoked salmon–lined terrine mold. Cover the mold with plastic wrap and refrigerate overnight until firm. Remove from the refrigerator, slice and serve.

MAKES 1 TERRINE

Ingredients

6		**large, ripe tomatoes**
3 cups •	750 mL	**extra virgin olive oil**
3 cloves		**garlic**
4		**bay leaves**
¼ cup •	50 mL	**sea salt**
2 Tbsp. •	30 mL	**star anise or fennel seeds**
2 cups •	500 mL	**carrot juice**
1 cup •	250 mL	**peach juice**
2 oz. •	60 g	**ginger, peeled and halved**
¼ cup •	50 mL	**Riesling**
		kosher salt and white pepper to taste
2 lbs. •	1 kg	**pickerel fillets, divided into 6 portions**
2 Tbsp. •	30 mL	**unsalted butter**
1 bunch		**watercress for garnish**

Pickerel with Tomato Confit
and Riesling Reduction

Confit is a dish from the Gascony region of France. The term refers to the method of preserving meat by first salting it then storing it in its own fat. Typically this means packing the meat in a crockpot and storing it for the lean winter months. In this recipe the tomato is cooked slowly in olive oil, spices and garlic to coax out its true flavor, which is a perfect foil for the fish. My use of the term "confit" is a way of paying homage to the traditional methods I respect; this recipe is not a true confit.

Preheat oven to 300°F (150°C).

Core the tomatoes and place in a small casserole just large enough to hold them. Pour in just enough olive oil to cover the tomatoes halfway up. Add the garlic, bay leaves, salt and star anise or fennel seeds. Cover and cook in the oven until tender and the tomato skins begin to peel, about 30 minutes.

Combine the carrot and peach juices with the ginger and bring to a boil. Stir in the Riesling and simmer until the juice has reduced by half and has thickened slightly. Remove the ginger and discard. Keep the sauce warm.

Remove the tomatoes from the confit and place on kitchen towel to catch the excess oil. Season the tomatoes with salt and pepper and transfer to 6 dinner plates.

Season the pickerel with salt and pepper. In a large sauté pan set over medium heat melt the butter. When the butter is frothy add the pickerel fillets, skin-side up. Cook for 5 minutes then turn the fillets over and cook for another 3 minutes. Carefully remove the fillets and balance each one atop a tomato. Top each piece of pickerel with some watercress and spoon the carrot peach reduction around the plates. Serve.

MAKES 6 SERVINGS

Ingredients

2 Tbsp.	·	30 mL	**green peppercorns, crushed**
2 Tbsp.	·	30 mL	**pink peppercorns, crushed**
2 Tbsp.	·	30 mL	**black peppercorns, crushed**
2 Tbsp.	·	30 mL	**white peppercorns, crushed**
½ cup	·	125 mL	**bread crumbs**
3 Tbsp.	·	45 mL	**grated Parmesan cheese**
2 Tbsp.	·	30 mL	**parsley, chopped**
1 Tbsp.	·	15 mL	**Dijon mustard**
2 Tbsp.	·	30 mL	**honey**
6			**boneless, skinless chicken breasts**
1 Tbsp.	·	15 mL	**olive oil**
2 Tbsp.	·	30 mL	**unsalted butter**

Chicken with Four Peppercorn Crust

This recipe shows that a Riesling with generous acidity and apple floral notes is the perfect wine to match with aggressive spices. Riesling wines are often recommended to accompany Asian-style foods and curry. In this case, the spice comes from the combination of 4 different peppercorns and a touch of Dijon mustard.

Combine the peppercorns with the bread crumbs, Parmesan cheese and parsley. Mix thoroughly and reserve.

Combine the mustard with the honey in a small bowl. Working with one chicken breast at a time, dip into the honey mustard mix then immediately into the peppercorn mix to coat the chicken. Repeat with the remaining chicken and reserve the coated breasts.

Preheat oven to 400°F (200°C).

Heat the olive oil and butter in a large sauté pan over medium heat. When the butter is frothy, add the chicken and sauté until golden brown on each side, about 6 minutes.

Transfer to the oven and cook for another 10 minutes. Serve immediately.

MAKES 6 SERVINGS

Ingredients

2 Tbsp.	·	30 mL	**olive oil**
2 Tbsp.	·	30 mL	**unsalted butter**
$\frac{1}{2}$ cup	·	125 mL	**onion, finely chopped**
$\frac{1}{2}$ cup	·	125 mL	**fennel, finely chopped**
2			**leeks (white part only), chopped**
1 cup	·	250 mL	**potato, peeled and diced**
2 cloves			**garlic, minced**
3 cups	·	750 mL	**sweet peppers, seeded and chopped**
1 tsp.	·	5 mL	**mild paprika**
1			**bay leaf**
$\frac{1}{2}$ tsp.	·	2.5 mL	**cayenne pepper (or to taste)**
$\frac{1}{2}$ cup	·	125 mL	**dry white wine**
4 cups	·	1 L	**Chicken Stock (page 267)**
$\frac{1}{2}$ cup	·	125 mL	**35% cream**
1 tsp.	·	5 mL	**white wine vinegar**
			kosher salt and white pepper to taste

Sweet Pepper Bisque

This is another recipe inspired by my experience as the executive chef of the Millcroft Inn Country House Hotel. I felt great pressure to live up to my predecessor's culinary standards. This soup was created out my respect and admiration for Chef Freddy Stamm.

In a large stockpot, heat the oil and add the butter. When the butter is frothy, add the onion, fennel, leeks and potato and cook for 10 minutes, stirring frequently. Add the garlic and the peppers.

Stir frequently for 5 minutes then add the paprika, bay leaf, cayenne pepper, white wine and chicken stock. Bring to a rapid boil then reduce the heat and simmer for 30 minutes, or until the vegetables are cooked through.

Transfer the soup to a food processor and purée until smooth. Strain through a sieve into a clean soup pot. Add the cream and return the soup to a gentle simmer. Reduce the heat and add the vinegar and salt and pepper. Serve in warmed bowls.

MAKES 6 SERVINGS

Ingredients

2 lbs. · 1 kg		**pork tenderloin, divided into 6 portions**
		kosher salt and white pepper to taste
1 Tbsp. · 15 mL		**olive oil**

Pork Tenderloin
with Niagara Succotash

I really learned to enjoy succo-tash when I worked for a short while in Virginia. It is a southern dish of sweet corn, tomato and lima beans. My version calls for fava beans and a little heat from a fresh jalapeño.

Preheat oven to 475°F (240°C).

Season the pork with the salt and pepper and rub with the olive oil. Place a sauté pan on high heat and sear the pork on all sides until golden brown (5–10 minutes).

Transfer the pork to an ovenproof dish and bake for 10 minutes, or to your preference.

Remove from the oven and keep warm.

MAKES 6 SERVINGS

Ingredients

1 Tbsp. ·	15 mL	**olive oil**
2 Tbsp. ·	30 mL	**unsalted butter**
1		**shallot, finely chopped**
1 clove		**garlic, finely chopped**
$\frac{1}{2}$		**jalapeño pepper, seeded and finely chopped (optional)**
$\frac{1}{2}$		**red pepper, seeded and finely chopped**
$\frac{1}{2}$ cup		**corn kernels, blanched**
$\frac{1}{2}$ cup ·	125 mL	**fava beans, blanched and peeled**
$\frac{1}{4}$ cup ·	50 mL	**white wine**
12		**large basil leaves (6 chopped and 6 for garnish)**
1		**ripe tomato, seeded and finely chopped**
		kosher salt and white pepper to taste

Niagara Succotash

Heat a medium saucepan over high heat and add the olive oil and butter.

When the butter is frothy add the shallot, garlic and jalepeño (if using) and cook for 5 minutes, stirring frequently. Add the sweet pepper, corn and fava beans and cook for another 5 minutes, stirring frequently. Add the white wine and reduce the liquid by half. Reduce heat to medium and add the chopped basil and the tomatoes. Season with salt and pepper.

Serve the succotash topped with sliced pork tenderloin and garnished with whole basil leaves.

Ingredients

6			**pickerel fillets (6 oz./175 g each) skin on and pin bones removed**
			kosher salt and white pepper to taste
½ cup	·	125 mL	**olive oil**

Pickerel
with Cucumber Noodles and Tomato Butter

This is a recipe I created for Christine Cushing's television show and it has been one of the more popular recipe requests we receive. I like to feature this dish during the summer months when the pickerel from Northern Ontario's lakes is pristine.

Season the pickerel with salt and pepper. Heat the olive oil in a pan over moderate heat and place the fish, skin-side up, in the oil. Flip the fish after 3 minutes and cook the other side for 2 minutes.

Remove from the heat and keep warm.

MAKES 6 SERVINGS

Ingredients

2			**English cucumbers, peeled and thinly sliced with a mandoline**
1 Tbsp.	·	15 mL	**granulated sugar**
2 Tbsp.	·	30 mL	**red wine vinegar**

Cucumber Noodles

Season the cucumbers with the sugar and red wine vinegar. Refrigerate until ready to serve.

Ingredients

2 Tbsp.	·	30 mL	**unsalted butter**
2 Tbsp.	·	30 mL	**olive oil**
3 leaves			**basil**
1 stalk			**celery, chopped**
1			**carrot, peeled and chopped**
1			**leek, washed and chopped**
1 clove			**garlic, chopped**
1 lb.	·	500 g	**fresh, ripe, red tomatoes**
1 cup	·	250 mL	**Riesling**
½ cup	·	250 mL	**cold butter, cubed**

Tomato Butter

In a small saucepan melt the butter with the olive oil and add the basil, celery, carrot, leek and garlic. Cook for 6 minutes, or until vegetables have softened. Add the tomatoes and bring to a quick boil. Add the white wine and simmer until the wine has evaporated, about 10 minutes.

Purée the sauce in a food processor, strain through a sieve and return the sauce to a small saucepan. Bring sauce to a boil, whisk in the cold butter and reserve.

Ingredients

| 2 lbs. | · | 1 kg | **mixed seasonal vegetables: cherry tomatoes, patti pan squash, leeks, asparagus, peas** |

for the vegetable medley

Steam the vegetables or blanch them, if you prefer, in chicken stock or water.

Spoon some tomato butter onto each of 6 large dinner plates. Place the vegetable medley on the center of the tomato butter. Place the fish atop the vegetable medley and garnish with little piles of the cucumber noodles.

Ingredients

2 lbs.	·	1 kg	**fresh ling cod, cut into 8 portions**
2 Tbsp.	·	30 mL	**olive oil**
			kosher salt and white pepper to taste
8 sprigs			**thyme, finely chopped**
1			**lemon, zest of, finely minced**

Ling Cod

with Oyster Mushroom Sauce and Mashed Potatoes

Ling cod is very much like halibut, but is underused. Eating white fish with mashed potatoes reminds me of a salted cod dish my mother used to make. She soaked the salted cod for 3 days in cold water then stewed the fish in tomato sauce and olives. Now that I mention it, doesn't it sound good?

Preheat oven to 400°F (200°C).

Place the cod on a roasting pan and drizzle the olive oil overtop. Season with salt and pepper and add the thyme and lemon zest. Cook the cod in the oven until the flesh feels slightly springy, about 8 minutes. Keep the fish warm.

MAKES 8 SERVINGS

Ingredients

2 Tbsp.	·	30 mL	olive oil
2 Tbsp.	·	30 mL	unsalted butter
2 lbs.	·	1 kg	oyster mushrooms
1 clove			garlic, minced
½ cup	·	125 mL	Riesling
¼ cup	·	50 mL	35% cream
1 tsp.	·	5 mL	Dijon mustard
1			green onion
			kosher salt and white pepper to taste

Oyster Mushroom Sauce

Heat a medium saucepan over medium heat and add the olive oil and butter. When the butter is frothy, add the oyster mushrooms and stir until they are quite wilted, about 10 minutes. Add the garlic and stir to combine. Add the wine, cream and mustard. Simmer the sauce until reduced by half and slightly thickened, about 10 minutes. Add the green onion and adjust the salt and pepper.

Ingredients

1 lb.	·	500 g	potatoes, peeled and cubed
			sea salt
3 Tbsp.	·	45 mL	olive oil
½ cup	·	125 mL	goat cheese
2 Tbsp.	·	30 mL	snipped chives

for the mashed potatoes

Place the potatoes in a large pot and cover with cold water. Set the pot over medium-high heat and cook the potatoes until soft, about 30 minutes. Transfer the potatoes to a food mill and process into a smooth mash. Add the olive oil, goat cheese and chives.

Serve the cod with the mushrooms on a bed of mashed potatoes.

Ingredients

4 cups	·	1 L	lobster, fish or Chicken Stock, or more as needed
$^3/_4$ cup	·	175 mL	olive oil
1			live lobster, about 2 lbs./1 kg
1			onion, peeled and finely chopped
$^3/_4$ cup	·	175 mL	Arborio rice
pinch			saffron
6 Tbsp.	·	175 g	unsalted butter
$^1/_2$ cup	·	125 mL	dry white wine
			kosher salt and white pepper to taste
2 Tbsp.	·	30 mL	butter
2 Tbsp.	·	30 mL	grated Parmesan cheese
2 Tbsp.	·	30 mL	minced chives

A Lobster Tasting Menu

Saffron Lobster Risotto

What could be more glamorous or luxurious than eating lobsters? I rank it right up there with foie gras, truffles, caviar and icewine as one of life's greatest culinary pleasures. Unlike those other ingredients, however, lobster remains quite accessible to most people as an occasional indulgence. These recipes are presented in honor of my wife, Kaleen, who is surely the greatest lover of lobster the world has ever seen.

Preheat oven to 500°F (260°C).

Pour the stock into a large stockpot and bring to a simmer. Keep stock simmering until required.

Heat $^1/_2$ cup (125 mL) of the olive oil in a roasting pan. Kill and season the lobster, add it to the roasting pan and roast it in the oven for 20 minutes, basting frequently. Remove from the oven and, when the lobster is cool enough to handle, remove the lobster meat from the shell.

Heat the remaining olive oil in a medium sauté pan and add the onion. Stir in the rice, saffron, butter and wine and stir until the oil has coated the kernels of rice and the rice is beginning to crackle. Add the hot stock in small increments until the rice has absorbed it all and is cooked *al dente*. Season with salt and pepper and fold in the butter and Parmesan. Stir to incorporate and serve, topped with the reserved lobster meat and minced chives.

MAKES 6 SERVINGS

*A Lobster
Tasting
Menu*

Ingredients

1 Tbsp. · 15 mL		**unsalted butter**
1		**shallot, minced**
$\frac{1}{2}$ cup · 125 mL		**Riesling**
2 Tbsp. · 30 mL		**lemon juice**
		kosher salt and white pepper to taste
$\frac{1}{2}$ lb. · 250 g		**fresh scallops (use either bay or sea)**
1		**egg white**
pinch		**nutmeg**
1 cup · 250 mL		**35% cream**
1 Tbsp. · 15 mL		**chopped chives**
2 tsp. · 10 mL		**lemon zest, finely chopped**
1 cup · 250 mL		**cooked lobster meat, cubed**

Lobster and Scallop Mousse
with Caviar Vinaigrette

Melt the butter in a sauté pan set over moderately high heat. Sauté the shallot in the butter for 3 minutes. Add the wine, lemon juice and salt and pepper and bring to a boil. Continue to boil until the liquid is reduced by half.

Transfer the scallops to a food processor and add the wine reduction, egg white and nutmeg. Purée until smooth, then add the cream and blend well. Combine the scallop purée with the lobster meat.

Butter four $\frac{1}{4}$-cup (50-mL) ramekins and divide the seafood mixture among them. Cover with plastic wrap and refrigerate overnight.

Preheat oven to 300°F (150°C). Place the ramekins in a bain-marie and bake for 1 hour or until the mousse is set. Remove from the oven and chill for 2 hours. To unmold, dip the molds into very hot water then invert onto a flat plate and serve with Caviar Vinaigrette (page 111).

MAKES 6 SERVINGS

Ingredients

¹⁄₄ cup	•	50 mL	**sherry vinegar**
1 Tbsp.	•	15 mL	**honey**
¹⁄₂ cup	•	125 mL	**grapeseed oil**
pinch			**kosher salt and white pepper to taste**
¹⁄₂ oz.	•	12 g	**caviar**

Caviar Vinaigrette

Mix all the ingredients, except the caviar, with a wire whisk.

Fold in the caviar and stir gently.

Ingredients

2 Tbsp. · 30 mL		**unsalted butter**
1		**small onion, finely diced**
½ cup · 125 mL		**green beans, blanched and cut into 1-inch (2.5-cm) pieces**
½ cup · 125 mL		**fava beans**
½ cup · 125 mL		**new potatoes, sliced**
¾ cup · 175 mL		**lobster or vegetable stock**
¼ cup · 50 mL		**35% cream**
		kosher salt and white pepper to taste
pinch		**cayenne pepper**
3 lbs. · 1.5 kg		**lobster meat, cut into 1-inch (2.5-cm) cubes**
2 Tbsp. · 30 mL		**tarragon, finely chopped**
1		**lemon, juice and zest of**
½ cup · 125 mL		**cherry tomatoes, or plum tomatoes, seeded and finely diced (concasse)**
12 leaves		**radicchio for garnish**

A Lobster Tasting Menu

Lobster Succotash

Melt the butter over medium heat, add the onion and cook for 5 minutes until tender. Add the green beans, fava beans, potatoes and lobster or vegetable stock. Reduce heat and simmer for 5 minutes. Add the cream and simmer for another 5 minutes.

Season with salt, pepper and cayenne. Add the lobster meat, tarragon, lemon juice and zest and tomato concasse. Stir to warm through the lobster and serve on radicchio leaves.

MAKES 6 SERVINGS

Ingredients

2 Tbsp. •	30 mL	**unsalted butter**
¹⁄₂ cup •	125 mL	**onion, chopped**
2 cups •	500 mL	**leeks (white part only), washed and chopped**
4 cups •	1 L	**salsify, peeled and chopped**
1 cup •	250 mL	**potatoes, peeled and chopped**
2		**lemons, zest and juice of**
6 cups •	1.5 L	**Chicken Stock (page 267)**
		kosher salt and white pepper to taste
1 Tbsp. •	15 mL	**olive oil**
18		**sea scallops**

Salsify Soup
with Pan-Seared Scallops

Salsify is an ugly vegetable with a wonderful taste reminiscent of oyster and coconut. For a visually interesting presentation, top each scallop with an olive or with mushroom purée.

Melt the butter in a heavy stockpot over moderate heat. Add the onion and leeks and cook until soft, about 10 minutes. Stir in the salsify, potatoes and lemon zest and cook for 3 minutes. Add the stock and bring to a boil. Reduce the heat to a simmer and cook until the vegetables are soft, 30 to 40 minutes.

Purée the soup in a blender until smooth. Add the lemon juice then taste and adjust the seasoning as necessary. Keep the soup warm.

MAKES 6 SERVINGS

for the scallops

Heat the olive oil in a non-stick sauté pan set over high heat. Season the scallops with salt and pepper then add them to the pan and sauté on each side for 90 seconds.

Divide the scallops among 6 soup bowls, ladle in the soup and serve.

Ingredients

¾ cup	• 175 mL	**Chicken Stock (page 267)**
½ cup	• 125 mL	**unsalted butter**
1		**lemon, in sections**
3 Tbsp.	• 45 mL	**capers**
2 Tbsp.	• 30 mL	**Italian parsley, finely chopped**
		kosher salt and white pepper to taste
½ cup	• 125 mL	**all-purpose flour**
2 tsp.	• 10 mL	**kosher salt**
2 tsp.	• 10 mL	**freshly ground white pepper**
pinch		**cayenne pepper**
1 tsp.	• 5 mL	**ground ginger**
3 lbs.	• 1.5 kg	**skate wings, cleaned and boned, cut into 6 steaks**
2 Tbsp.	• 30 mL	**unsalted butter**
2 Tbsp.	• 30 mL	**olive oil**

Skate
with Caper Brown Butter Sauce

Skate, or skate wing, is a fish from the same family as shark. Like shark, skate should not have any ammonia smell when you buy it. The scent of ammonia is a sure sign of poor handling or an old product. This delicious meat should be purchased skinned and de-boned. Use skate in any crab recipe; its versatility and delicious flavor will impress you.

In a small saucepot over medium heat bring the chicken stock to a boil and reduce by half. Reserve.

Meanwhile, in another small saucepot, melt the butter until it is foamy, then cook it for 5 minutes, or until it turns brown. Remove the butter from the heat. Gradually add the reduced chicken stock, whisking to emulsify the butter. Remove the sections of the lemon and squeeze the remaining pith to extract 1–2 Tbsp. (15–30 mL) of juice. Add the lemon juice, the lemon sections, capers and Italian parsley. Season with salt and pepper and reserve.

Combine the flour, salt, pepper, cayenne and ginger. Dip each skate wing into the seasoned flour and shake off the excess. In a large sauté pan over medium-high heat melt the butter in the olive oil. Add the skate to the pan and fry for 5 minutes or until the fish is golden brown. Turn and cook the other side for another 3–6 minutes, or until the fish is cooked through.

Serve the skate topped with brown butter on 6 warmed dinner plates.

MAKES 6 SERVINGS

Ingredients

2½ lbs. ·	1.25 kg	**pork tenderloin, cut into 6 portions**
3 Tbsp. ·	45 mL	**olive oil**
		kosher salt and white pepper to taste
1 clove		**garlic, finely diced**
1		**shallot, finely diced**
6 ears		**fresh corn, kernels of**
½		**red bell pepper, seeded and cut into 1-inch (2.5-cm) dice**
½		**yellow pepper, seeded and cut into 1-inch (2.5-cm) dice**
¼ cup ·	50 mL	**white wine**
½ cup ·	125 mL	**35% cream**
1 tsp. ·	5 mL	**cayenne pepper**

Smoked Pork Loin
with Riesling Creamed Corn and Fritters

Smoking food adds a layer of flavor which, depending on the wood used for the smoke, lends either a complementing or contrasting flavor to the product being smoked. Riesling wine, especially an older one, seems to have an affinity for the smoke because it mirrors the earth, minerals and petrol flavors smoking imparts.

Brush the pork with 2 Tbsp. (30 mL) of the olive oil, season with salt and pepper and refrigerate. When you're ready, smoke the pork according to the instructions on page 119.

In a sauté pan over medium heat, warm the remaining olive oil and add the garlic and shallots. Add the corn and peppers and sauté for a few minutes without allowing the vegetables to color.

Add the white wine and simmer until reduced by half. Add the cream, bring to a simmer and season to taste with salt, pepper and cayenne. Keep warm.

MAKES 6 SERVINGS
recipe continued on page 119

HOW TO PAN-SMOKE MEAT

To make a stovetop smoker you will need a cast iron pan. Combine dried wood chips, herb stems and peppercorns, and soak in water or wine for 1 hour.

Place the cast iron pan on a very hot element and heat until it's smoking.

Drain the liquid from the soaking wood chips, herb stems and peppercorns and add them to the hot cast iron pan. Be careful not to let the water/steam scald you. Place a piece of aluminum foil over the smoking wood/herbs and lay the meat down on top of the aluminum foil. Cover the meat with another sheet of aluminum foil and allow to smoke for 15 minutes (or longer if a stronger smoke flavor is desired). When the meat is done, carefully remove the top layer of aluminum foil then lift out the meat and continue with the recipe. Discard the spent wood chips/herbs in the smoker.

Ingredients

3 cups	750 mL	**oil for deep frying**
$\frac{1}{2}$ cup	125 mL	**pastry flour**
$\frac{3}{4}$ cup	175 mL	**all-purpose flour**
1 tsp.	5 mL	**salt**
2 tsp.	10 mL	**baking powder**
2 tsp.	10 mL	**ground ginger**
2		**eggs, well beaten**
2 Tbsp.	30 mL	**maple syrup**
2 cups	500 mL	**milk**
2		**apples, peeled, cored and diced**
$\frac{3}{4}$ cup	175 mL	**pecans, roughly chopped**
		kosher salt and white pepper to taste

for the fritters

Heat the oil in a deep fat fryer to 350°F (180°C).

Combine the pastry flour, all-purpose flour, salt, baking powder and ginger and reserve.

In a mixing bowl, blend the eggs, maple syrup and milk. Add the apple and pecans. Add the flour mixture to the egg/apple mixture and blend until well incorporated. Season the batter with salt and pepper.

Spoon the batter into the hot oil and cook until golden brown, about 5 minutes.

Lift the fritters out of the oil onto kitchen towel to absorb excess oil.

Serve the fritters with smoked pork tenderloin and Riesling creamed corn.

Ingredients

3		**eggs, slightly beaten**
generous pinch		**saffron**
		kosher salt and white pepper to taste
2 tsp. •	10 mL	**dill, chopped**
1		**lemon, juice and zest of**
1½ lbs. •	750 g	**salmon, cut into 6 pieces, skin and bones removed**
2 Tbsp. •	30 mL	**unsalted butter**
2 Tbsp. •	30 mL	**olive oil**

Saffron Salmon
with Pine Nut Apple Salad

In this recipe, a saffron-scented egg marinade turns into a crust when it's cooked, resulting in a very moist piece of fish. Try this technique with halibut for a beautiful color contrast. I serve it with an easy salad where autumn's apples steal the show. Saffron is a particularly good match to a young Riesling, especially one with a forward palate of citrus and honey.

Combine the eggs, saffron, salt and pepper, dill, lemon juice and zest in a bowl. Add the salmon and refrigerate for 3 hours.

In a medium sauté pan (preferably non-stick), melt the butter in the olive oil over medium heat. Add the chilled salmon, one piece at a time, and sauté until the egg coating has become golden brown all over the fish, about 10 minutes.

Remove from the heat and reserve.

MAKES 6 SERVINGS

Ingredients

½		**red onion, finely sliced**
½		**fennel bulb (white parts only), finely sliced**
1 cup •	250 mL	**mushrooms, sliced**
1		**lemon, juice of**
½ tsp.		**ginger, peeled and minced**
1 clove		**garlic, finely chopped**
1 Tbsp. •	15 mL	**cilantro, finely chopped**
½ cup •	125 mL	**pine nuts, toasted**
2		**apples, cored, peeled and chopped**
1 Tbsp. •	15 mL	**champagne vinegar**
3 Tbsp. •	45 mL	**olive oil**

for the salad

Combine all the salad ingredients and serve immediately with the sautéed salmon.

Ingredients

2 Tbsp.	· 30 mL	**unsalted butter**
2 Tbsp.	· 30 mL	**olive oil**
1		**onion, chopped**
2		**leeks (white parts only), chopped**
2 tsp.	· 10 mL	**garlic, chopped**
4 cups	· 1 L	**parsnips, peeled and chopped**
1 lb.	· 500 g	**Yukon Gold potatoes, peeled and cubed**
3 cups	· 750 mL	**ripe pears, peeled, cored and chopped**
8 cups	· 2 L	**Chicken or Mushroom Vegetable Stock (pages 267, 43)**
6		**sage leaves**
3 sprigs		**rosemary**
		kosher salt and white pepper to taste

Pear and Parsnip Soup

I first combined these flavors when I was a sous chef at Langdon Hall Country House Hotel. We served it to our guests after they'd spent an afternoon snowshoeing through the forest. I often find that combining familiar flavors in a new way satisfies healthy appetites.

In a large heavy-bottomed stockpot, melt the butter in the olive oil over medium heat. Add the onion, leek and garlic, and cook for 10 minutes, stirring frequently to prevent any coloring. Add the parsnip, potatoes and pear. Stir and cook for 5 minutes, or until the vegetables soften.

Pour in the chicken or vegetable stock to just cover the vegetables.

Bring to a rapid boil, reduce the heat and simmer until the potatoes are cooked through. Add the fresh herbs, salt and pepper and cook for 5 minutes longer.

Remove from the heat and drain off the stock. Reserve the stock.

In a food processor purée the vegetables until smooth. Transfer the purée back to a clean soup pot over moderate heat. Gradually add the reserved stock until you reach the desired soupy consistency. When the soup comes to a simmer, adjust the seasonings and serve.

MAKES 6 SERVINGS

Ingredients

1 Tbsp.	•	15 mL	**olive oil**
1 Tbsp.	•	15 mL	**unsalted butter**
1½ lbs.	•	750 g	**fresh halibut fillets (cut into 6 servings)**
			kosher salt and white pepper to taste

Roasted Halibut
with Sweet Potato Purée and Pickled Onions

This recipe is beautiful in its simplicity. A perfectly moist roasted halibut steak is perched on top of a light cloud of sweet potato purée. The acidity of the pickled onions is the perfect complement to balance the overall effect of culinary harmony.

Preheat a medium saucepan over moderately high heat. Heat the olive oil and butter, but not to the point of smoking. Season the fish with salt and pepper and add it to the pan, flesh-side down. Cook the fish for 5 minutes then turn it and cook the other side for a further 4 minutes.

to serve

Arrange the sweet potato purée (page 125) on the center of warmed dinner plates. Place the fish on the purée and arrange the pickled onions (page 125) around the fish and serve.

MAKES 6 SERVINGS
recipe continued on next page

Ingredients

1		**large sweet potato, halved horizontally**
1 Tbsp. •	15 mL	**unsalted butter**
1 Tbsp. •	15 mL	**white truffle oil**
		kosher salt and white pepper to taste

Sweet Potato Purée

Preheat oven to 375°F (190°C).

Place the sweet potatoes, skin-side down, in an ovenproof dish or tray and bake for 30 minutes. Turn the potatoes and bake for a further 20 minutes, or until easily pierced with a fork.

Remove the potatoes and, when they are cool enough to handle, scoop out the flesh and mix with the butter, truffle oil, salt and pepper. Stir until the butter has completely melted into the mixture and reserve.

Ingredients

1		**red onion, sliced into $\frac{1}{2}$-inch (1-cm) rings**
$\frac{1}{2}$ cup •	125 mL	**red wine**
$\frac{1}{2}$ cup •	125 mL	**red wine vinegar**
1 clove		**garlic, minced**
1 tsp. •	5 mL	**mustard seed, toasted**
1 tsp. •	5 mL	**fennel seed, toasted**
2 tsp. •	10 mL	**kosher salt**
1		**bay leaf**

Pickled Onions

Combine all the ingredients and refrigerate for 24 hours (place a weight on the onions so they are fully submerged).

Ingredients

1 Tbsp.	• 15 mL	**olive oil**
2 Tbsp.	• 30 mL	**unsalted butter**
1		**red onion, thinly sliced**
2		**Belgian endive, thinly sliced**
1 lb.	• 500 g	**smoked chicken**
½ cup	• 125 mL	**green onions, thinly sliced**
½ cup	• 125 mL	**Riesling**
2 tsp.	• 10 mL	**garlic purée**
4 cups	• 1L	**cooked noodles, such as penne, linguine or pappardelle**
½ cup	• 125 mL	**walnut halves**
		kosher salt and white pepper to taste
½ cup	• 125 mL	**Italian parsley, chopped**

Smoked Chicken Pasta
with Walnuts, Endive and Parsley

You can really taste wine country in this recipe. The sauce is made from a splash of Riesling, some roasted garlic and a touch of butter. This is the real taste of terroir.

In a large sauté pan set over medium heat warm the olive oil and butter.

When the butter is frothy add the onion and the endive. Stir until the onions are slightly browned, about 3 minutes. Add the smoked chicken and the green onions. Add the wine and simmer until the liquid is reduced by half. Stir in the garlic purée. Add the pasta and the walnuts. Toss until well blended.

Season to tase with salt and pepper and garnish with parsley. Serve immediately.

MAKES 6 SERVINGS

Ingredients

2 Tbsp. •	30 mL	**unsalted butter**
2 lbs. •	1 kg	**veal loin, cut into 6 pieces**
		kosher salt and white pepper to taste
40 cloves		**blanched garlic (page 129)**
1 cup •	250 mL	**Riesling**
6 sprigs		**thyme**
6 sprigs		**rosemary**

Veal Baked with 40 Cloves of Garlic

Do not attempt this recipe unless you are cooking for garlic lovers. I am not kidding. However, in this recipe, its power is harnessed by repetitive blanching and slow cooking in olive oil. This produces sweet and creamy garlic, a perfect match to a veal loin.

In a small ovenproof sauté pan set over medium-high heat melt the butter.

Season the veal with salt and pepper and when the butter is frothy, add the veal to the sauté pan. Sear the meat on each side until golden brown, but still uncooked, for about 1 minute per side. Remove the veal and keep it warm.

Preheat oven to 400°F (200°C).

Add the blanched garlic and Riesling to the sauté pan and let the wine reduce until it has almost all evaporated. Return the veal to the pan and sprinkle with the herbs. Place the sauté pan in the oven and cook the veal for approximately 10 minutes, or to your preference.

Remove from the oven and serve with the garlic.

MAKES 6 SERVINGS

Ingredients

40 cloves		**garlic, peeled**
6 cups	• 1.5 L	**water**
1 cup	• 250 mL	**olive oil**

for the blanched garlic

Divide the water among 3 small pots and bring each to a rapid boil. Plunge the garlic into the first pot and, as soon as the water returns to a boil, remove it with a slotted spoon and immediately plunge it into a bowl of ice water. When the garlic has cooled thoroughly, repeat the process in the other 2 pots of boiling water, discarding the water after each use.

Transfer the boiled garlic to a kitchen towel and let air dry for 30 minutes.

Preheat oven to 300°F (150°C).

Transfer the garlic to a small ovenproof pot and add just enough olive oil to cover. Place the pot in the oven and cook for 2 hours or until the garlic is completely soft but retains its shape. Reserve.

Spring

Roasted Fennel Soup

Grilled Salmon
  with Herbed Vegetable Topping

Shrimp and Scallops
  in Roasted Garlic Cream Sauce

Barbecued Quail
  with Grilled Asparagus
  Potato Salad

Summer

Potato and Pesto Soup

Herb-Marinated Goat Cheese Ravioli

Composed Salad of Garden Beans
  with Blueberry Vinaigrette

Grilled Chicken
  with Celery Root, Escarole and Apples

Chardonn

THE CHARDONNAY GRAPE PRODUCES THE WORLD'S MOST FAMOUS wine. It is suited to the growing conditions in many countries and is produced in just about every wine region of the world. It is a variety loved by wine makers for its vinicultural flexibility. At its worst it can be sweet and overly oaked, but at its best it can be made into a dry wine with magnificent bouquets, nice acidity and a refreshing, clean taste.

Chardonnay can be fruity and light, or oaky and big with butterscotch, honey, butter, vanilla, apple, pear

Autumn

Pumpkin Bisque
   with Glazed Chestnuts

Gnocchi
   with Roasted Chestnuts and
   Sweet Potato Sauce

Maritime Mussels
   with Chorizo, Wild Rice and Chardonnay

Braised Romaine Lettuce
   with Prosciutto, Peppers and
   Anchovy Dressing

Turkey Breast Noisettes
   with Chardonnay Grape Stuffing

Winter

Buttercup Squash Soup

Salmon with Potato Crust
   and Dried Peach Salad

Slow-Roasted Pheasant
   with Chardonnay Braised Mushrooms

ay

and clove flavors. From a culinary standpoint, Chardonnay can be challenging. Foods intended to be consumed with Chardonnay should be simple and direct. Some foods, such as mushrooms and truffles, seem an obvious choice to be paired with an oak-aged wine. Lighter and medium-bodied wines seem suited to vegetables such as fennel and peas. Too many flavors on the plate will compete with the many nuances of flavor in the glass, so keep things simple.

Chardonnay can also be a full-bodied, full-character wine, which at its best matches with many dishes ranging from game birds to turkey burgers and seafood. I enjoy the culinary challenge of integrating Chardonnay into our repertoire of recipes. It is a grape variety which is perfectly suited to my cuisine. The complexities of an excellent Chardonnay complement the simplicity and full-flavored approach to my wine country cuisine.

Ingredients

2 Tbsp.	· 30 mL	**olive oil**
1 Tbsp.	· 15 mL	**unsalted butter**
1		**onion, chopped**
1 clove		**garlic, chopped**
1 tsp.	· 5 mL	**fennel seed**
3 bulbs		**roasted fennel (page 133)**
6 cups	· 1.5 L	**Chicken Stock (page 267)**
$^1/_2$ cup	· 125 mL	**35% cream**
		kosher salt and white pepper to taste

Roasted Fennel Soup

There is no vegetable quite like fennel. With a clean, crisp and refreshing taste, it is a pleasure to cook with, eat and serve. It has the reputation of having a strong licorice taste but it has more in common with mint. When choosing fennel, choose the bulbs that are shiny and white with no blemishes, and look for the bright green leaves (fronds).

Heat the olive oil and butter in a soup pot over medium heat. Add the onion and cook until soft, about 5 minutes. Add the garlic and continue to cook, stirring constantly, for 30 seconds. Add the fennel seed and the roasted fennel and stir.

Add the chicken stock and increase the heat to high. Bring to a boil, then reduce the heat to a simmer. Cook for 15–20 minutes until the fennel is very tender. Remove from the heat and let cool.

Transfer the soup to a food processor and purée until smooth. Strain the soup through a fine mesh strainer into a clean pot. Return to medium-high heat and bring to a boil. Add the cream and stir until well blended. Season to taste with salt and pepper and serve.

MAKES 6 SERVINGS

for the roasted fennel

Ingredients

¼ cup · 50 mL		olive oil
2		lemons, juice of
1		bay leaf
2 sprigs		thyme
2 sprigs		rosemary
3		fennel bulbs (white parts only), quartered

Preheat oven to 350°F (180°C).

Combine the olive oil, lemon juice, bay leaf, thyme and rosemary in a bowl. Add the fennel and stir to combine. Place the
fennel on a baking sheet and bake for 30 minutes or until it
becomes golden brown around the edges and is soft. Turn the
fennel over and cook for anther 30 minutes until cooked
through. Reserve.

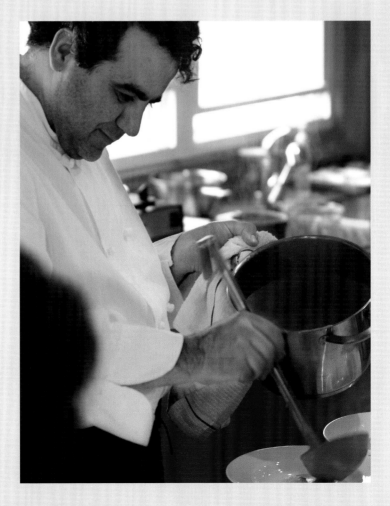

Ingredients

1		zucchini, cut into $1/2$-inch (8-mm) slices
1		red bell pepper, seeded and quartered
1		yellow bell pepper, seeded and quartered
1		red onion, sliced into $1/2$-inch (8-mm) rings
4		green onions
1		fennel bulb, trimmed and quartered
4		portobello mushrooms, halved
2 heads		red radicchio, halved
		kosher salt and white pepper to taste
1 Tbsp.	15 mL	Dijon mustard
1		lemon, juice of
2 Tbsp.	30 mL	Chardonnay
1 tsp.	5 mL	minced garlic
$1/2$ cup	125 mL	olive oil
1 cup	250 mL	bread crumbs
2 sprigs		rosemary, finely chopped
2 sprigs		tarragon, finely chopped
$1/4$ cup	50 mL	chives, finely chopped
2 lbs.	1 kg	salmon, divided into 6 portions
2 Tbsp.	30 mL	olive oil

Grilled Salmon
with Herbed Vegetable Topping

Grilled salmon is one of life's simple pleasures. Its rich flavor is a perfect match for the golden brown smokiness of a grill. I love cooking salmon over charcoal and when I do, I put the lid down over the grill to lock in all that smoke flavor. Make the vegetable topping a day in advance for added flavor.

Preheat the grill. Toss the vegetables together and season with salt and pepper. Add the mustard, lemon juice, wine, garlic and the $1/2$ cup (125 mL) of olive oil. Grill the vegetables until they have developed golden brown grill marks, about 10 minutes.

When the vegetables have cooled enough to handle, pulse them in a food processor. Transfer the vegetable purée to a bowl and add the bread crumbs, rosemary, tarragon and chives.

Sprinkle the salmon with salt and pepper and rub with a nice coating of olive oil. Place the salmon on the grill and cook to your preferred doneness. (I suggest 6 minutes per side.) When the salmon is cooked, top generously with the herbed vegetable topping and serve.

MAKES 6 SERVINGS

Ingredients

1		shallot, finely chopped
1 clove		garlic, finely chopped
2 sprigs		cilantro, finely chopped
1		lemon, juice and finely chopped zest of
¼ cup	• 50 mL	olive oil
¼ cup	• 50 mL	Chardonnay
1		bay leaf
		kosher salt and white pepper to taste
1 tsp.	• 5 mL	chipotle pepper
12		black tiger shrimp (13–15 count), peeled and deveined
12		sea scallops

Shrimp and Scallops
in Roasted Garlic Cream Sauce

Do you want to impress your guests so much that they will bother you for weeks to get this recipe? In all of my years of experience, I have been never been so tempted to dip my finger in any sauce as when we make this recipe in the restaurant. This combination of delicately roasted garlic infused with sweet cream and the subtle sharpness of grainy mustard is intoxicating. Scallops and shrimp are the ideal accompaniment to this sauce, but try it with fresh halibut or even with rabbit and noodles for terrific results.

Combine the ingredients for the marinade and pour over the shrimp and scallops. Cover with plastic wrap and refrigerate.

Remove the shrimp and scallops from the marinade and pat dry. Season with salt and pepper and place in the reserved cream sauce. Bring the sauce back to a simmer and cook until the shrimp is pink and the scallops are cooked through. Adjust the seasoning and serve.

MAKES 6 SERVINGS
recipe continued on next page

Chef's Tip

If more liquid is needed (if the sauce appears too thick), add a touch of white wine or water.

Ingredients

2 Tbsp.	• 30 mL	**olive oil**
2 Tbsp.	• 30 mL	**unsalted butter**
2		**shallots, finely chopped**
2 cloves		**roasted garlic**
1 tsp.	• 5 mL	**ginger, peeled and finely chopped**
1/2 cup	• 125 mL	**icewine**
1/2 cup	• 125 mL	**35% cream**
2 Tbsp.	• 30 mL	**grainy mustard**
2 tsp.	• 10 mL	**champagne vinegar**
		kosher salt and white pepper to taste

Roasted Garlic Cream Sauce

In a small saucepot, heat the olive oil and butter over medium heat. Add the shallots and cook until they are translucent, about 2 minutes. Stir in the roasted garlic and the ginger, and cook for 5 minutes, stirring frequently. Add the icewine and cream and bring to a boil. Reduce the heat to a simmer and cook until the sauce coats the back of a wooden spoon. Add the mustard and vinegar and stir. Season with salt and pepper.

Pour the sauce through a sieve and keep warm.

Ingredients

6		**quail, boneless**
¼ cup	• 50 mL	**Quail Barbecue Marinade (page 140)**
30 spears		**asparagus, peeled**
½ cup	• 125 mL	**Chardonnay**
3		**potatoes, halved and blanched**
2		**red onions, cut into rings**
6 sprigs		**rosemary, chopped**
6 sprigs		**thyme, chopped**
6 sprigs		**parsley, chopped**
½ cup	• 125 mL	**olive oil**
2 Tbsp.	• 30 mL	**unsalted butter**
		kosher salt and white pepper to taste

Barbecued Quail
with Grilled Asparagus Potato Salad

What better way to celebrate spring than with a backyard barbecue? Surprise your friends by preparing this easy recipe for barbecued quail. This recipe is ideal for entertaining because the vegetable herb packages can be made ahead of time and the quail only needs 5 minutes per side on the grill for perfection.

Place the quail in a small casserole and cover with the marinade. Refrigerate for 1 hour.

Preheat the barbecue to moderately high. Combine all the remaining ingredients in a large bowl and toss. Season with salt and pepper.

Cut out 6 pieces of aluminum foil roughly 12 inches x 12 inches (30 cm by 30 cm) and lay them flat on a counter.

Divide the tossed vegetables among the 6 foil squares. Bring up the corners of the aluminum foil to seal and place in the barbecue. Cook for 15 minutes and remove from the heat.

Meanwhile, remove the quail from the marinade, season with salt and pepper, then place on the grill. Cook for 5 minutes on each side. Remove the quail from the grill.

To serve, rip open the aluminum foil parcels and transfer the vegetables to large dinner plates. Top with the quail and serve.

MAKES 6 SERVINGS

recipe continued on next page
photograph on page 141

Ingredients

2 Tbsp. ·	30 mL	**olive oil**
1		**onion, sliced thinly**
1 clove		**garlic, minced**
2 Tbsp. ·	30 mL	**maple syrup**
1 Tbsp. ·	15 mL	**black peppercorns, crushed**
1 tsp. ·	5 mL	**tomato paste**
1 tsp. ·	5 mL	**chili flakes**
½ cup ·	125 mL	**Chardonnay**
½ cup ·	125 mL	**Chicken Stock (page 267)**
¼ cup ·	50 mL	**cider vinegar**

Quail Barbecue Marinade

In a small saucepan heat the olive oil over medium-high heat and add the sliced onion. Reduce the heat and stir frequently until the onion is golden brown, about 10–15 minutes. Add the garlic and stir to combine with the onion. Add all the remaining ingredients except the cider vinegar and bring to a boil.

Reduce the heat and simmer the marinade until it reduces by half. Strain the marinade through a fine mesh sieve and let cool. When the marinade has cooled to room temperature add the cider vinegar.

Ingredients

¼ cup	• 50 mL	**vegetable oil**
3		**onions, sliced**
2 cloves		**garlic, minced**
6		**potatoes, peeled and chopped**
1 cup	• 250 mL	**Chardonnay**
6 cups	• 1.5 L	**Chicken Stock (page 267)**
		kosher salt and white pepper to taste

Potato and Pesto Soup

As a young boy, I thought it was cool to have dirt under my finger-nails from harvesting summer potatoes. We used to bring in bushels of them to be part of summer meals. Now that I'm older, I love the feeling of the moist dirt in my hands when I dig for potatoes. There's no better way to keep yourself grounded than the physical labour of digging up potatoes. This recipe is an adaptation of a rustic soup my mother used to make.

Heat the oil in a large soup pot over moderate heat. Add the onions and cook for 10 minutes, stirring frequently, until the onions have softened. Add the garlic. When the garlic has softened, add the potatoes, wine and stock. Bring to a boil, reduce the heat and simmer for 45 minutes or until the potatoes are cooked through.

Season with salt and pepper.

Purée the soup, using a hand-held blender or a food processor, until smooth. Strain the soup through a fine mesh sieve and return to the soup pot. Bring to a boil and adjust seasoning.

Keep the soup warm.

to serve

Pour the potato soup into heated soup bowls and spoon in the pesto. Use a spoon to swirl the pesto around to infuse with the potato soup. Serve.

MAKES 6 SERVINGS

Ingredients

1 cup	· 250 mL	**fresh basil**
2 Tbsp.	· 30 mL	**roasted garlic**
$^1\!/_2$ cup	· 125 mL	**pine nuts, lightly toasted**
2 Tbsp.	· 30 mL	**grated Parmesan cheese**
$^3\!/_4$ cup	· 180 mL	**olive oil**

Pesto

There are many versions of this classic ancient Northern Italian sauce. Some recipes call for garlic, while others omit the nuts. What separates this recipe from other pesto recipes is the roasted garlic (as opposed to raw garlic, which can impart bitterness to the sauce) and the toasted pine nuts which give it a nuttier, deeper flavor.

Combine the ingredients in a food processor and purée until smooth. Remove the pesto from the food processor. Reserve until ready to use.

Ingredients

1 recipe			**Semolina Pasta Dough (page 174)**

for the goat cheese filling

$\frac{1}{4}$ cup	·	50 mL	**extra virgin olive oil**
2 tsp.	·	10 mL	**thyme, finely chopped**
2 tsp.	·	10 mL	**rosemary, finely chopped**
2 tsp.	·	10 mL	**chives, finely chopped**
1 tsp.	·	5 mL	**coriander, finely chopped**
1 Tbsp.	·	15 mL	**Italian parsley, finely chopped**
1 tsp.	·	5 mL	**black peppercorns, crushed**
2 tsp.	·	10 mL	**pink peppercorns, crushed**
$\frac{3}{4}$ lb.	·	340 g	**goat cheese**
2 Tbsp.	·	30 mL	**unsalted butter**
1 Tbsp.	·	15 mL	**olive oil**
1 clove			**garlic, chopped**
2			**shallots, finely chopped**

Herb-Marinated Goat Cheese Ravioli

Don't be intimidated by the prospect of making fresh pasta. The satisfaction of eating fresh noodles is worth the effort. This recipe is beautiful in its simplicity and you will truly appreciate the quality of the ingredients.

In a small casserole, mix the olive oil with the herbs and peppercorns. Place the goat cheese in a bowl. Pour the olive oil and herb mix over the goat cheese and refrigerate overnight.

In a medium sauté pan, melt the butter over medium-high heat and add the olive oil. When the butter has melted, add the garlic and shallots and cook, stirring occasionally, for 5 minutes or until the vegetables are soft. Remove from the heat and cool to room temperature. Transfer to a medium bowl and refrigerate.

When they have cooled, mix the shallots and garlic with the goat cheese until smooth. Fill according to instructions on next page.

MAKES TWENTY-FOUR $2\frac{1}{2}$-INCH (6-CM) RAVIOLI

EVERYTHING YOU NEED TO KNOW ABOUT MAKING RAVIOLI BUT
WERE AFRAID TO ASK!

1. Roll the dough out to a thin sheet, roughly $5\frac{1}{2}$ inches
    wide and 16 inches long (13 cm by 40 cm).

2. Cut the sheet of dough in half.

3. Cover one half with a damp tea towel to keep it from
    drying out.

4. Along the length of the uncovered dough, place 1 Tbsp.
    (15 mL) of filling in a neat ball 1 inch (2 cm) from the
    bottom and side edges, and 1 inch (2 cm) apart.

5. Have a small bowl of water ready.

6. With your finger moisten the bottom edge and the spaces
    between each ball of filling.

7. Place the other dough sheet over the ravioli filling so that
    the edges meet evenly.

8. Using the edges of your hands, flatten and seal the spaces
    between each ball of filling as close as possible to the filling,
    expelling any pockets of air at the unsealed end.

9. Press the bottom and top edges together to seal.

10. Use a ravioli wheel cutter or a knife to cut out the ravioli,
    cutting right through both sheets, to create $2\frac{1}{2}$-inch (6-cm)
    squares.

11. To cook the ravioli, immerse them in a pot full of salted,
    boiling water.

12. When they float to the top and the edges are soft, after
    about 5 minutes, remove them with a slotted spoon and
    serve.

Ingredients

2 Tbsp.	•	30 mL	**sherry vinegar**
³⁄₄ cup	•	175 mL	**olive oil**
1			**shallot, chopped**
2			**tomatoes, peeled and finely diced**
2 Tbsp.	•	30 mL	**chives, chopped**
1 Tbsp.	•	15 mL	**chervil, chopped**
1 tsp.	•	5 mL	**tarragon, chopped**
½ cup	•	125 mL	**green beans, blanched**
½ cup	•	125 mL	**yellow beans, blanched**
1 cup	•	250 mL	**Blueberry Vinaigrette (page 148)**

Composed Salad of Garden Beans
with Blueberry Vinaigrette

You may question the unusual combination of green beans and blueberries in this visually appealing salad but it is a taste experience that will pleasantly surprise you. Serve this salad with a fruit forward Chardonnay, perhaps one aged in stainless steel or minimal oak.

Mix the vinegar with the olive oil in a bowl and add the chopped shallot, tomatoes and herbs. Stir to combine. Place the blanched beans in another bowl and pour in half the vinaigrette. Reserve the remaining half.

MAKES 6 SERVINGS
recipe continued on next page

Ingredients

1		**potato, peeled**
3 Tbsp. ·	45 mL	**melted butter**
		kosher salt and white pepper to taste
1 bunch		**fresh herbs of your choice**

for the herbed potato chips

Preheat oven to 375°F (190°C).

Using a very sharp vegetable slicer, carefully slice the potato into very thin, almost translucent, slices. Place half the potato slices on a non-stick baking sheet and brush them with melted butter. Place a herb sprig on the center of each potato and season with salt and pepper. Cover the sprig with another layer of potato.

Brush with the butter again and bake until the chips are crispy and brown, about 15 minutes.

Ingredients

½ cup ·	125 mL	**fresh blueberries**
½ cup ·	125 mL	**reserved vinaigrette (page 147)**
1		**lemon, juice only**
pinch		**granulated sugar**

Blueberry Vinaigrette

Process the blueberries in a blender until smooth. Add the vinaigrette and the lemon juice. Strain the mixture and add the sugar.

Spoon the blueberry vinaigrette onto each plate. Build towers with alternating layers of potato chips and garden beans and serve.

Grilled Chicken
with Celery Root, Escarole and Apples

When cooking with wine we sometimes invent recipes using a technique called "echoing" to match the dominant flavor of the recipe to the dominant flavor of the wine. For this recipe choose a refreshing Chardonnay with silky smooth apple flavors and a medium body.

Ingredients

6			**chicken breasts, 6 oz./175 g each**
$\frac{1}{2}$ cup	•	125 mL	**olive oil**
1 Tbsp.	•	15 mL	**cracked black peppercorns**
2 Tbsp.	•	30 mL	**thyme, chopped**
2 Tbsp.	•	30 mL	**rosemary, chopped**
1 tsp.	•	5 mL	**chili flakes**

Remove the skin from the chicken. In a medium bowl combine the olive oil, peppercorns, thyme, rosemary and chili flakes. Add the chicken to the bowl and completely cover both sides of the chicken with the marinade then refrigerate.

MAKES 6 SERVINGS

recipe continued on next page

Ingredients

1 cup	· 250 mL	**celery root, peeled and julienned**
2		**apples, peeled, cored and julienned**
1		**lemon, juice and blanched zest of**
2 oz.	· 50 g	**pancetta, finely diced**
2 tsp.	· 10 mL	**Dijon mustard**
2 Tbsp.	· 30 mL	**35% cream**
2 Tbsp.	· 30 mL	**mayonnaise (page 13)**
2 Tbsp.	· 30 mL	**chives, finely chopped**
		kosher salt and white pepper to taste
3		**escarole lettuces**

for the salad

Mix together the celery root and the apples and add the lemon juice and zest. In a sauté pan set over medium heat cook the pancetta for about 10 minutes. When the pancetta is golden brown remove it and pat dry with kitchen towel. Add the pancetta to the apple/celery root mix. Add the mustard, cream, mayonnaise and chives, and mix well.

Season with salt and pepper to taste. Reserve.

Preheat oven to 375°F (190°C).

Remove the chicken from the marinade. Discard the marinade and place the chicken in the oven on a baking sheet. Cook for 6 minutes on each side or until juices run clear and chicken is cooked all the way through.

Divide the escarole among 6 salad plates. Top the greens with the celery root salad. Place the cooked chicken on the salad.

Serve.

Ingredients

2 Tbsp. ·	30 mL	**olive oil**
1		**onion, sliced**
2		**leeks (white part only), chopped**
2 cups ·	500 mL	**reserved pumpkin flesh**
2 cloves		**garlic, finely chopped**
2		**potatoes, peeled and cubed**
6 cups ·	1.5 L	**Chicken Stock (page 267)**
1 herb sachet		**thyme, bay leaf, rosemary**
		kosher salt and white pepper to taste

Pumpkin Bisque
with Glazed Chestnuts

Pumpkins are one reason I look forward to fall every year. The many varieties make it possible to integrate them into endless recipes. One of my favorite ways to use them is in soups.

Choose any variety of pumpkin available in your area, but try to choose small ones with no blemishes and which seem too heavy for their size.

In a large heavy-bottomed soup pot set over medium-high heat warm the olive oil. Add the onion and the leeks and cook until the vegetables have softened, about 5 minutes. Add the reserved pumpkin flesh (page 153) and stir.

Cook for 5 minutes, stirring frequently, then add the garlic and potatoes. Add the chicken stock and bring to a boil. Add the herb sachet and simmer until the vegetables have cooked through, about 15 minutes. Pass the soup through a strainer, and reserve the liquid, discarding the herb sachet.

Transfer the solids of the soup to a food processor and purée until smooth. Transfer the purée back to the soup pot and add some of the reserved liquid to achieve the desired consistency. Bring the soup to a boil over high heat. Reduce the heat, simmer for 10 minutes and season to taste with salt and pepper. Garnish with Glazed Chestnuts (page 153) and serve.

MAKES 6 SERVINGS

Ingredients

3			**small pumpkins, halved**
2 cups	•	500 mL	**Chardonnay**
½ cup	•	125 mL	**unsalted butter**
			kosher salt and white pepper to taste

for the roasted pumpkin

Preheat oven to 350°F (180°C).

Place the pumpkins in a roasting pan sliced-side down, leaving the seeds in them. Pour the Chardonnay over the pumpkins. Cut the butter into small cubes and sprinkle over the pumpkins. Bake in the oven for 2 hours or until the pumpkin is cooked through. Remove from the oven and let cool.

When the pumpkin is cool enough to handle, scoop out the seeds and discard.

Remove the cooked flesh from the pumpkins and discard the skins. You should have about 2 cups (500 mL) of pumpkin.

Ingredients

12			**whole chestnuts**
½ cup	•	125 mL	**Chicken Stock (page 267)**
1 Tbsp.	•	15 mL	**unsalted butter**
1 Tbsp.	•	15 mL	**granulated sugar**
			kosher salt and white pepper to taste

Glazed Chestnuts

My dad used to roast chestnuts in our fireplace and the smell would delight my entire family. When I got older, my parents would let me prepare them, so I'd leave one or two uncut just so the popping sound would startle my mom.

Preheat oven to 400°F (200°C).

Make an incision into the chestnuts to prevent them from popping. Place them on a baking sheet and cook for 20 minutes. Remove from the oven and peel them while they are still hot.

Place half of the chicken stock, all of the butter, the sugar and the seasonings in a small saucepan and cook over medium heat until the liquid has reduced to 2 Tbsp. (30 mL). Add the remaining chicken stock and cook for another 10 minutes until the chestnuts are glazed and cooked through.

Ingredients

2 lbs.	•	1 kg	**russet or baking potatoes**
1 cup	•	250 mL	**all-purpose flour (more as needed)**
2 tsp.	•	10 mL	**kosher salt**
2 cups	•	500 mL	**spinach, washed, blanched and chopped**
2			**eggs**
1 cup	•	250 mL	**ricotta cheese**
1 Tbsp.	•	15 mL	**sage, chopped**
2 Tbsp.	•	30 mL	**olive oil**
2 Tbsp.	•	30 mL	**grated Parmesan cheese**
1 recipe			**Sweet Potato Sauce (page 156)**
			roasted chestnuts (page 153)

Gnocchi with Roasted Chestnuts
and Sweet Potato Sauce

My kids love making gnocchi. It was a great way for me to teach them about the rewards of hard work. I first started making these dumplings in my mother's restaurant many years ago and this is still one of my favorite recipes. Chestnuts may seem like an intimidating ingredient, but the joy created by the smell of chestnuts roasting in your home will outweigh the chore of the finicky task.

Preheat oven to 400°F (200°C).

Bake the potatoes until a metal skewer slides easily through them, 45 minutes to an hour. Hold the hot potatoes, one at time, with a pot holder or kitchen towel and peel with a paring knife or vegetable peeler. Use a potato masher or ricer to mash them in a large bowl. Sprinkle the flour and 1 tsp. (5 mL) salt over the potatoes. Add the spinach, eggs, ricotta and sage. Using your hands, work the mixture into a soft, smooth dough. If the dough is sticky, add more flour as needed.

Roll about one quarter of the dough into a long 1-inch (2.5-cm) rope. Cut the dough rope into 2-inch (5-cm) lengths. Holding a fork in one hand, press each piece of dough against the ridged surface of the fork and with your index finger make an indentation in the center of each gnocchi. Roll the dough off the end of the fork and allow it to drop to the work surface.

Fill a large pot with water and bring it to a boil. Add salt to taste. Add about one-third of the gnocchi and cook until they float, 1 to 2 minutes. Repeat with remaining gnocchi. Retrieve the cooked gnocchi with a slotted spoon and transfer to a warm, shallow serving bowl or platter. When all the gnocchi are cooked, drizzle with olive oil and sprinkle with grated Parmesan cheese. Keep warm.

MAKES 6 SERVINGS

recipe continued on next page

Ingredients

2 Tbsp. •	30 mL	**olive oil**
2 Tbsp. •	30 mL	**unsalted butter**
1		**shallot, finely chopped**
1 clove		**garlic, chopped**
2		**sweet potatoes, peeled and chopped**
1 Tbsp. •	15 mL	**honey**
$\frac{1}{2}$ cup •	125 mL	**tomato, seeded and finely chopped**
2 sprigs		**thyme, chopped**
1 sprig		**rosemary, chopped**
3 leaves		**sage, chopped**
2 cups •	500 mL	**Chicken or Mushroom Vegetable Stock (pages 267, 43)**
2 tsp. •	10 mL	**truffle oil**
		kosher salt and white pepper to taste

Sweet Potato Sauce

In a small saucepot heat the olive oil to medium-high. Add the butter and when it is frothy add the shallot and garlic. Reduce the heat to moderate and stir frequently until the shallot has browned slightly, about 3 minutes.

Add the sweet potatoes, honey, tomato, herbs and stock. Cover and bring to a boil. Reduce the heat and simmer until the sweet potato is cooked through, about 30 minutes. Transfer the contents of the pot to a food processor or blender and process until smooth. Return the sauce to the pot and bring to a simmer. Whisk in the truffle oil and add salt and pepper to taste.

to serve

Place a small puddle of truffled sweet potato sauce on each warm dinner plate.

Place a portion of gnocchi on each puddle of sauce and top with a few scattered roasted chestnuts.

Garnish with more fresh Parmesan and sage, if desired.

Ingredients

2 Tbsp. •	30 mL	**olive oil**
2 Tbsp. •	30 mL	**unsalted butter**
1 cup •	250 mL	**sliced chorizo sausage**
1		**red onion, julienned**
$\frac{1}{2}$ cup •	125 mL	**cooked wild rice**
2 cloves		**garlic, finely minced**
3 lbs. •	1.5 kg	**fresh mussels**
$\frac{1}{2}$ cup •	125 mL	**Chardonnay**
$\frac{1}{2}$ cup •	125 mL	**35% cream**
2 Tbsp. •	30 mL	**unsalted butter**
$\frac{1}{2}$ cup •	125 mL	**green onions, finely chopped**
		kosher salt and white pepper to taste

Maritime Mussels
with Chorizo, Wild Rice and Chardonnay

This delicious recipe is inspired by the incomparable Spanish dish paella. Here the mussels are the star of the show. The wild rice and sausage are not only there for taste but also for an intriguing textural component.

Heat a large sauté pan over medium-high heat and add the olive oil and 2 Tbsp. (30 mL) butter.

When the butter is frothy, add the chorizo and cook, stirring frequently, for about 10 minutes. When the sausage has lightly browned, add the onion. Reduce the heat to medium and, when the onions have browned slightly, add the wild rice, garlic and mussels. Add the Chardonnay and cover the pan.

Cook until the mussels open slightly, about 2 minutes.

Add the cream and 2 Tbsp. (30 mL) butter and cover the pan again until the butter has melted. Add the green onions and remove from the heat when the mussels have completely opened. Season with salt and pepper and serve.

MAKES 6 SERVINGS

Ingredients

2 Tbsp. •	30 mL	**olive oil**
1		**shallot, finely chopped**
1 clove		**garlic, finely chopped**
3		**hearts of romaine, halved lengthwise**
¼ cup •	50 mL	**Chardonnay**
2 tsp. •	10 mL	**sherry vinegar**
2 sprigs		**rosemary**
1 recipe		**Anchovy Dressing (page 159)**
1 recipe		**prosciutto and red pepper garnish (page 159)**

Braised Romaine Lettuce
with Prosciutto, Peppers and Anchovy Dressing

The idea behind this recipe was to create a new version of the classic Caesar salad. The end result is this version, served warm, which first appeared on our fall menu in 1998 and continues to be a popular item. Look for romaine lettuce that is not blemished, with tightly wrapped leaves. Romaine hearts will give a more subtle and satisfying result.

Preheat oven to 350°F (180°C).

Using a large ovenproof sauté pan over medium-high heat, heat the olive oil and add the shallots and garlic. When the shallots have softened, after about 3 minutes, add the romaine hearts to the pan. Add the Chardonnay, vinegar and rosemary. Cover the lettuce with a lid or a piece of aluminum foil.

Place in the oven and braise for 10 minutes (or just until the lettuce wilts but does not lose its bright green color).

Remove from the oven and discard the aluminum foil. Pour the anchovy dressing overtop and let the romaine rest for 5 minutes. Divide the romaine hearts among 6 warm salad plates and sprinkle with the prosciutto and red pepper garnish.

MAKES 6 SERVINGS

Ingredients

¼ cup	•	50 mL	**olive oil**
3 Tbsp.	•	45 mL	**sherry vinegar**
1 Tbsp.	•	15 mL	**anchovy fillets**
2 tsp.	•	10 mL	**granulated sugar**

Anchovy Dressing

Combine all the ingredients and stir to emulsify. Reserve.

Ingredients

¼ cup	•	50 mL	**black olives, pitted**
1 Tbsp.	•	15 mL	**lemon zest, blanched**
6 slices			**prosciutto, cut into thin strips**
2			**medium red peppers, roasted, peeled, seeded and julienned**

for the garnish

Combine all the ingredients and reserve.

Ingredients

¼ cup	• 50 mL	**olive oil**
2 lbs.	• 1 kg	**turkey breast, skin removed, divided into 6 medallions**
		kosher salt and white pepper to taste
18		**sage leaves**
2 Tbsp.	• 30 mL	**unsalted butter**

Turkey Breast Noisettes
with Chardonnay Grape Stuffing

I am very proud of this dish because I believe it makes a significant contribution to Niagara's regional wine country cuisine. It's a beautiful fall dish that perfectly captures the aura of our terroir. The combination of turkey with grape stuffing is an example of how we bring the vineyard to the table. A balance of locally produced raw ingredients, excellent wine and a little culinary imagination.

Preheat oven to 375°F (190°C).

Roll out 6 pieces of aluminum foil and fold into 12-inch by 1-inch (30-cm by 2-cm) collars.

Rub the turkey with 2 Tbsp. (30 mL) of the olive oil and sprinkle with salt and pepper. Lay 2 sage leaves on each collar and fold the collars around the turkey pieces. In a heavy-bottomed sauté pan set over medium-high heat warm the remaining olive oil and the butter.

When the butter is frothy, add the turkey and sauté for 6 minutes per side. Transfer the pan to the oven and cook for 10 minutes or until a meat thermometer reads 160°F (75°C).

Remove from the oven and let the noisetes rest for 5 minutes.

to serve

Remove the foil collars from the noisettes, top with Chardonnay Grape Stuffing and serve.

MAKES 6 SERVINGS

Ingredients

3 Tbsp.	• 45 mL	**olive oil**
2		**shallots, finely chopped**
1 clove		**garlic, finely chopped**
1 cup	• 250 mL	**seedless grapes, halved**
1 cup	• 250 mL	**bread crumbs**
4 Tbsp.	• 60 mL	**chopped parsley**
		kosher salt and white pepper to taste

Chardonnay Grape Stuffing

Heat a sauté pan to moderate heat and add the olive oil. Add the shallots and garlic and sauté until soft, about 3 minutes. Add the grapes and stir. Remove from the heat and reserve.

In a small bowl combine the bread crumbs with the parsley. Season with salt and pepper. Combine the grapes with the bread crumbs and stir to combine well.

Ingredients

¼ cup	•	50 mL	**olive oil**
1			**onion, sliced**
2			**leeks (white part only), chopped**
3 cups	•	750 mL	**squash, peeled and chopped**
2 cloves			**garlic, finely chopped**
3			**Yukon gold potatoes, peeled and chopped**
6 cups	•	1.5 L	**Chicken Stock (page 267)**
1 herb sachet			**thyme, bay leaf, rosemary**
			kosher salt and white pepper to taste

One morning our forager, John Laidman, walked in with what surely was one of the ugliest vegetables I'd ever seen. All the cooks gathered around the counter and

Buttercup Squash Soup

stared at it. John split the mystery vegetable in half to reveal the beautiful, vivid orange flesh of what turned out to be a blue banana squash. Its taste (we tasted it raw) was nutty and lingering. This "ugly" has spoiled me from using common squashes ever again, but this recipe works fine with whatever squash you choose.

In a large heavy-bottomed soup pot, heat the olive oil. Add the onion and leeks and cook until the vegetables have softened, about 5 minutes. Add the squash and stir. Cook for 5 minutes, stirring frequently, then add the garlic and potatoes. Add the chicken stock and bring to a boil. Add the herb sachet, reduce the heat and simmer until the vegetables have cooked through, about 10 minutes. Pass the soup through a strainer, reserving the liquid and discarding the herb sachet.

Transfer the soup to a food processor and purée until smooth. Return the purée to the soup pot and add some of the reserved liquid. Add just enough to achieve the desired soup consistency. Bring the soup to a boil over high heat. Reduce the heat, simmer for 10 minutes and season to taste with salt and pepper.

Serve with a small amount of Goat Cheese Cream.

MAKES 6 SERVINGS

Ingredients

½ cup	•	125 mL	**goat cheese**
½ cup	•	125 mL	**35% cream**

Goat Cheese Cream

In the bowl of a stand mixer, combine the two ingredients and mix at medium speed until well combined. Using a rubber spatula, scrape into a container and refrigerate until required.

MAKES 1 CUP/250 ML

Ingredients

2 lbs.	•	1 kg	salmon fillet, divided into 6 equal portions
			kosher salt and white pepper to taste
1			potato, peeled and thinly sliced
¼ cup	•	50 mL	melted butter
2 Tbsp.	•	30 mL	olive oil

Salmon with Potato Crust
and Dried Peach Salad

This recipe depicts a harmonious balance of ingredients at the peak of their flavors. Products delivered to the kitchen by our forager in the early morning are often featured on the day's menus and showcase the affinity between Hillebrand's VQA wines and our regional cuisine.

Preheat oven to 400°F (200°C).

Sprinkle the salmon with salt and pepper. Toss the thinly sliced potato in melted butter and season with salt and pepper. Place the potato slices on the salmon fillets in an overlapping fashion until the top surface of the salmon is completely covered with the potato.

Add the olive oil to an ovenproof non-stick sauté pan set over moderately high heat. Add the salmon fillets with the potato-side down in the hot oil. Sauté for 3 minutes.

Transfer the pan to the oven and bake for 10 minutes. Remove from the oven and keep warm.

to serve

Remove the peach sections from the cabbage mixture. On 6 warmed dinner plates, arrange the peach sections in a circular fashion (12 o'clock, 2 o'clock, 4 o'clock etc.). Divide the rest of the cabbage mixture among the plates. Place the salmon on the cabbage mixture and serve with the potato-side up. Drizzle any liquid left from the cabbage mixture around the plates

Garnish with fresh snipped chives and serve.

MAKES 6 SERVINGS

recipe continued on next page

Ingredients

¼ cup	• 50 mL	**unsalted butter**
3 Tbsp.	• 45 mL	**olive oil**
1		**shallot, peeled and finely diced**
2 tsp.	• 10 mL	**ginger, finely minced**
3 Tbsp.	• 45 mL	**dried peaches, finely chopped**
2 cups	• 500 mL	**Savoy cabbage, julienned**
1 cup	• 250 mL	**Fish Stock (page 50)**
½ cup	• 125 mL	**Chardonnay**
3		**fresh peaches, cut into 8 pieces**
1 cup	• 250 mL	**fresh corn kernels, blanched**
		kosher salt and white pepper to taste

Dried Peach Salad

In a large sauté pan set over moderate heat, melt the butter with the olive oil. When the butter is frothy, add the shallot, ginger and dried peaches. Stir frequently then add the cabbage, fish stock and Chardonnay.

When the wine and stock have reached boiling point, reduce the heat to medium and simmer. Cover the cabbage with a lid or aluminum foil and let it cook until all the moisture has evaporated. Add the fresh peaches, corn kernels, salt and pepper.

Stir and continue cooking until the fresh peaches are warmed through.

Remove from the heat and keep warm.

Ingredients

1 Tbsp. •	15 mL	**black peppercorns**
4		**juniper berries**
1 Tbsp. •	15 mL	**mustard seeds**
2 tsp. •	10 mL	**thyme, finely chopped**
1 tsp. •	5 mL	**rosemary, chopped**
1 tsp. •	5 mL	**ginger, peeled and finely chopped**
2 Tbsp. •	30 mL	**olive oil**
3		**whole pheasants, breasts and legs removed from the carcasses**
		kosher salt to taste
3 Tbsp. •	45 mL	**olive oil**
2 Tbsp. •	30 mL	**butter, cut into small pieces**

Slow-Roasted Pheasant
with Chardonnay Braised Mushrooms

I think pheasant is a great option for those who want to eat poultry but are tired of chicken. With its slightly darker meat and a richer, deeper flavor, pheasant is a perfect match to a full-bodied, oaked Chardonnay. The Chardonnay braised mushrooms are perfumed by the wine reduction and the nice tang of Dijon mustard and crème fraîche make this dish a classic Chardonnay match.

Combine the peppercorns, juniper berries and mustard seeds in a spice mill and grind until coarse. Mix the spices with the fresh herbs, ginger and 2 Tbsp. (30 mL) of olive oil.

Combine the pheasant breasts and legs with the spice/herb mix in an ovenproof baking dish. Cover with plastic wrap and refrigerate for 1 hour. Remove the pheasant from the refrigerator and sprinkle with the 3 Tbsp. (45 mL) of olive oil.

Preheat oven to 350°F (180°C).

Cook in the oven for 20 minutes or until the pheasant breast is cooked through, then remove them from the oven and keep warm.

Continue cooking the legs for another 20–25 minutes or until cooked through.

While the pheasant is cooking, begin the Chardonnay Braised Mushrooms.

MAKES 6 SERVINGS

Ingredients

3 Tbsp. · 45 mL	**olive oil**
2 oz. · 50 g	**pancetta, finely diced**
1	**onion, chopped**
1 cup · 250 mL	**carrot, julienned**
2 Tbsp. · 30 mL	**unsalted butter**
1 clove	**garlic**
3 cups · 750 mL	**winter mushrooms, cleaned and chopped**
1 cup · 250 mL	**Chardonnay**
1 cup · 250 mL	**Chicken Stock (page 267)**
1 Tbsp. · 15 mL	**Dijon mustard**
2 Tbsp. · 30 mL	**crème fraîche (page 79)**
	kosher salt and white pepper to taste

Chardonnay Braised Mushrooms

In an ovenproof saucepan, heat the olive oil. Add the pancetta and stir frequently until it turns slightly brown. Add the onion and carrot and the butter. Stir frequently until the onion and carrot are shiny and have softened, about 5 minutes. Add the garlic, mushrooms and Chardonnay.

Stirring frequently for 35 to 45 minutes, reduce the Chardonnay until about 2 Tbsp.(30 mL) remains. Add the chicken stock.

Preheat oven to 350°F (180°C). Cover the pan with a lid or aluminum foil and place in the oven. Braise the mushrooms for 1 hour or until half the liquid remains in the pan and the mushrooms have softened considerably.

Remove the pan from the oven and stir in the mustard. Add the crème fraîche. Season with salt and pepper to taste.

Transfer the mushrooms to a serving platter and top with the roasted pheasant. Serve one leg and half a breast per guest.

Spring

Beef Carpaccio
with St. Ann's Goat's Milk Cheese,
Asparagus and Almonds

Ravioli
with Pancetta, Chicken and Rosemary

Salmon
with Wild Rice, Morels and Wild Leeks

Summer

Roasted Eggplant and Red Pepper Soup

Grilled Pork Tenderloin
with Peach Salsa

Thyme Roasted Quail
with Garlic Sauce and Venturi-Schulze
Balsamic Vinegar

Wine Country Spareribs

Gamay No

I REMEMBER WHEN I WAS A YOUNG COMMIS DE CUISINE, working in a country house hotel in England alongside a brigade of Frenchmen and listening to their anticipation of the annual release of the Beaujolais Nouveau. The anticipation they felt was tangible and exciting and it was contagious. I begged to be a part of the team that squeezed itself in a tiny Ford Fiesta (there were five of us), and drove through the night after a 15-hour work-day, to the town of Dover. There we would receive the first shipment from Calais of the precious Beaujolais Nouveau. In truth, we only saved ourselves 6 hours because by the time we got back to work the next day, the sommelier of the hotel had already received it and, to his amusement, let us know in no uncertain terms that we were *fou*.

Autumn

Baked Vegetable
and Oka Cheese Pan Bread

Duck Confit and Quinoa Tarts
with Sweet Onion Jam

Pan-Seared Sweetbreads
in Clover Honey with Apple Tomato
Chutney

Winter

Divinely Inspired White Bean Soup

Green Lentil Tapenade
with Cumin-Scented Sour Cream

Roasted Duck
with Sweet and Sour Sauce

Truffle Roasted Capon
with Gamay Noir Mushroom Sauce

ir

Gamay Noir is the black-skinned grape of the Beaujolais area of Burgundy, France, where it accounts for almost all of the vines. It is a variety of grape which, when grown in ideal soil conditions of granite and limestone soil with sandy clay (like in Beaujolais and in some areas of the Niagara peninsula), can grow quite vigorously. Its early bud break is subject to early frost sensitivity and it is often one of the first grapes to be harvested in mid-August to September. It is a wine best consumed young to maximize the enjoyment of its light and refreshing character. Gamay Noir is a grape that produces medium-bodied wines with fruity flavors such as strawberry, raspberry and cherry. It often has aromas ranging from violets and rose petals to banana and bubblegum.

This low-tannin, high-acidity wine is nicely balanced with subtle black pepper and spice and, when treated to moderate oak aging, can yield a bigger body with flavors of smoky vanilla and toast. Like the famous Beaujolais Nouveau from France, Niagara Gamay Noir is a pleasure to have on the dinner table. Gamay Noir's unique characteristics make wine suitable for a broad range of food-matching possibilities such as dishes using quail, chicken, pork, pasta and even fish and shellfish. Check out the Gamay Noir menu for pairing and cooking opportunities with my wine country cuisine.

Ingredients

¼ cup	•	50 mL	**olive oil**
1 lb.	•	500 g	**beef sirloin**
			kosher salt and white pepper to taste
1 Tbsp.	•	15 mL	**thyme, finely chopped**
1 Tbsp.	•	15 mL	**rosemary, finely chopped**
1 Tbsp.	•	15 mL	**sage, finely chopped**
1 Tbsp.	•	15 mL	**Dijon mustard**
1			**shallot, finely chopped**
2 Tbsp.	•	30 mL	**aged balsamic vinegar**

Beef Carpaccio
with St. Ann's Goat's Milk Cheese, Asparagus and Almonds

This recipe was created to showcase the wonderful goat cheese made by the C'est Bon dairy. It is a great example of the strides made by artisanal cheese makers to capture their terroir through their cheese. Carpaccio is the name of a classic Italian antipasto made traditionally from thinly sliced raw beef.

In a sauté pan set over medium-high heat, warm the olive oil. Season the beef with salt and pepper to taste. Add the beef and sear all sides until nicely charred. Remove from the pan and set on a large piece of plastic wrap.

Mix together the thyme, rosemary, sage, Dijon mustard, shallot and balsamic vinegar to form a paste. Spread this over the beef to completely coat. Wrap securely in the plastic and place in the freezer until the meat is almost totally frozen, for 8 hours or overnight.

Remove the meat from the freezer and allow to thaw partially. Using a very sharp knife, carefully slice the meat into 6 equal portions, then slice each portion into 5 or 6 very thin slices.

MAKES 6 SERVINGS

Ingredients

1 Tbsp.	·	15 mL	**capers, rinsed and finely chopped**
1 Tbsp.	·	15 mL	**grated Parmesan cheese**
36 spears			**asparagus, blanched**
36			**black olives, pitted**
1 Tbsp.	·	15 mL	**Italian parsley, chopped**
2 Tbsp.	·	30 mL	**sliced almonds, lightly toasted**
1			**lemon, juice of**
2 Tbsp.	·	30 mL	**olive oil**
			kosher salt and white pepper to taste
¼ cup	·	50 mL	**goat cheese**

for the salad

Combine all the ingredients except the goat cheese and season
to taste with salt and pepper.

Place the sliced beef carpaccio on 6 large dinner plates with a
small pile of salad in the middle. Crumble the goat cheese
over top and serve.

Ingredients

1 recipe			**Semolina Pasta Dough (page 174)**
for the filling			
4			**chicken legs**
			kosher salt and white pepper to taste
2 Tbsp.	·	30 mL	**olive oil**
2 Tbsp.	·	30 mL	**rosemary, finely chopped**
2 cloves			**garlic, thinly sliced**
4 oz.	·	125 g	**pancetta, diced**
1 tsp.	·	5 mL	**cracked black pepper**
1 Tbsp.	·	15 mL	**grated Parmesan cheese**

Ravioli with Pancetta, Chicken
and Rosemary

What better way to enjoy rich complementary flavors than to make delicate stuffed ravioli filled with chicken, pancetta and rosemary? A delight at any time of the year, during the spring we like to serve them with a delicate sauce made with only garlic-scented rosemary oil.

Preheat oven to 375°F (190°C).

Season the chicken legs with salt and pepper and toss with the olive oil and rosemary. Transfer the chicken to an oven-proof baking sheet and bake for 40 minutes, turning once after 20 minutes. At this point add the garlic and pancetta to the pan, distributing evenly over the chicken.

When the chicken is cooked through, transfer it to a cutting board. When cool enough to handle, remove the meat from the bones and dice, along with the pancetta and garlic, to a fine texture. Season with pepper and Parmesan and reserve.

Fill the ravioli according to the instructions on page 145.

to serve

Cook the ravioli in plenty of salted, boiling water until they rise to the surface, about 5 minutes. Drain and transfer to a large bowl. Toss the ravioli in the rosemary oil (see next page), season with salt and pepper and serve immediately.

MAKES 6 SERVINGS

recipe continued on next page

Ingredients

½ cup	• 125 mL	**extra virgin olive oil**
3 sprigs		**rosemary**
3 cloves		**garlic, crushed**
1 tsp.	• 5 mL	**black peppercorns**
1 tsp.	• 5 mL	**red chili flakes**
2 tsp.	• 10 mL	**fleur de sel**

for the rosemary oil

In a small saucepan, over medium heat, warm the olive oil, rosemary and garlic.

When the garlic is surrounded by small bubbles, add the peppercorns, red chili flakes and fleur de sel.

Ingredients

1½ cups	• 375 mL	**unbleached flour, plus additional for dusting**
1½ cups	• 375 mL	**durum semolina**
4		**large eggs, at room temperature**
½ tsp.	• 2 mL	**olive oil**
2 Tbsp.	• 30 mL	**water, or as needed**

Semolina Pasta Dough

In a food processor fitted with a metal blade, pulse the flour and the semolina for about 40 seconds to combine.

In a small measuring cup mix the eggs and olive oil. With the machine running add the egg mixture and then the water, just until the dough comes together into a mass, about 1 minute. If it feels too soft and sticky add a tablespoon (15 mL) or so of flour. If it is dry and crumbly, add some more water, a tablespoon (15 mL) at a time.

Remove the dough and knead it on a lightly floured surface until smooth and resilient, about 10 minutes. Wrap the dough in plastic wrap until required.

Ingredients

2 Tbsp.	•	30 mL	**olive oil**
2 Tbsp.	•	30 mL	**unsalted butter**
1			**onion, finely chopped**
1 clove			**garlic, finely chopped**
¹/₂ cup	•	125 mL	**wild rice**
1 cup	•	250 mL	**Chicken Stock (page 267) or water**
1 Tbsp.	•	15 mL	**rosemary, chopped**
1 Tbsp.	•	15 mL	**chives, chopped**
2 Tbsp.	•	30 mL	**chervil, chopped**
			kosher salt and white pepper to taste

Salmon with Wild Rice,
Morels and Wild Leeks

This innovative recipe exemplifies the barrier-busting possibilities of red wine with fish. A medium-bodied Gamay Noir is the wine of choice when wild spring salmon hits the market in early spring. This delicious fish is leaner than the typical farm-raised salmon, making it the star of this spring inspired recipe.

Heat the oil and butter in a small saucepan over moderately high heat. When the butter is frothy add the onions and garlic, stirring. Add the rice and sauté for a few minutes to completely coat it in the butter and oil. Add the stock or water and bring to a boil. Reduce the heat to a simmer and cook until the rice is soft, about 35–45 minutes. Remove from the heat.

Add the herbs and season with salt and pepper. Reserve.

MAKES 6 SERVINGS
recipe continued on next page

Ingredients

1.5 lbs.	750 g	**salmon divided into 12 equal portions (2 pieces each)**
2 Tbsp.	30 mL	**olive oil**
2 Tbsp.	30 mL	**unsalted butter**
2		**shallots, finely chopped**
1 clove		**garlic, finely chopped**
2 cups	500 mL	**morel mushrooms**
½ cup	125 mL	**Gamay Noir**
½ cup	125 mL	**Chicken Stock (page 267)**
2 Tbsp.	30 mL	**35% cream**
36		**wild leeks, cleaned**
1 Tbsp.	15 mL	**thyme, finely chopped**
1 Tbsp.	15 mL	**chives, finely minced**
1		**lemon, juice of**
		kosher salt and white pepper to taste
18		**baby carrots, cooked (optional)**

for the morels and wild leeks

Preheat oven to 375°F (190°F).

In a medium sauté pan, heat the olive oil and butter over moderately high heat until the butter is frothy. Add the salmon, skin side up, for 5 minutes, or until lightly browned. Remove from heat and reserve. Add the shallots and garlic and cook until the shallots are translucent, about 5 minutes. Add the morel mushrooms, Gamay Noir and chicken stock. Bring to a rapid simmer and let the wine reduce until 1 Tbsp. (15 mL) remains and the mushrooms have softened, about 10 minutes.

Add the 35% cream and bring to a simmer, stirring to incorporate the cream. Add the wild leeks, thyme, chives and lemon juice and season with salt and pepper. Place the salmon in the oven for 3–5 minutes until cooked through but still pink.

Divide the rice between 6 large dinner plates. Top each pile of rice with the salmon and spoon the morel mushroom and wild leeks around the plate. Add cooked baby carrots for garnish if desired.

Ingredients

3		eggplants, halved, flesh side scored in a criss-cross fashion
¼ cup	• 50 mL	kosher salt
½ cup	• 125 mL	olive oil
		kosher salt and white pepper to taste
2 Tbsp.	• 30 mL	unsalted butter
1		onion, finely diced
2 Tbsp.	• 30 mL	garlic, finely diced
2		leeks (white part only), finely diced
1 lb.	• 500 g	potatoes, peeled and finely diced
6		red peppers, halved, seeded and chopped
6 leaves		sage
3 sprigs		rosemary, chopped
4 cups	• 1L	Chicken Stock (page 267)

Roasted Eggplant
and Red Pepper Soup

In the late summer, when the farmers' fields have yielded their precious produce, I like to make this soup with two vegetables you may not think have much in common: eggplant and red pepper. In this recipe, not only do they tango, they also blend well and taste great.

Preheat oven to 400°F (200°C).

Sprinkle the eggplant with the kosher salt and let sit for an hour. Rinse the eggplant under a stream of cold water to remove the excess salt. Pat dry and sprinkle with olive oil and salt and pepper to taste. Put in the oven, skin-side down, and cook for 35 minutes, or until the flesh is slightly browned. Remove from the oven, let cool, then scrape out the flesh into a stainless steel bowl and discard the skin.

In a large heavy-bottomed stockpot, melt the butter over medium-high heat. Add the onion and stir. Cook until the onion is wilted but not colored. Add the leek, potato, red pepper and garlic. Stir and cook for 5 minutes. Add the eggplant and continue to cook for 5 minutes. Pour in the chicken stock to just cover the vegetables. Bring to a rapid boil, reduce the heat and simmer until the potatoes are cooked through, about 15 minutes. Add the fresh herbs and salt and pepper.

Remove from the heat and drain off the stock into a large bowl. In a food processor, purée the vegetables until smooth. Gradually add back the reserved stock until you reach the desired consistency.

Season with salt and pepper and serve in heated bowls.

MAKES 6 SERVINGS

Ingredients

¼ cup	50 mL	**olive oil**
2 tsp.	10 mL	**parsley, finely chopped**
1 tsp.	5 mL	**thyme, finely chopped**
1 tsp.	5 mL	**rosemary, finely chopped**
1 tsp.	5 mL	**summer savory, finely chopped**
1 Tbsp.	15 mL	**cracked black pepper**
1		**lemon, juice and zest of**
1		**shallot, finely chopped**
1 clove		**garlic, finely chopped**
2 lbs.	1 kg	**pork tenderloins, cut into 6 portions**

Grilled Pork Tenderloin
with Peach Salsa

Peaches are one of summer's treasures. Pork seems to have an affinity to fresh fruit flavors like peach, so we combined them in this easy summer recipe. Gamay Noir is the perfect summer wine because of its easy drinking and refreshing nature.

Combine all the ingredients, except the pork tenderloin, in a bowl and stir to combine.

Add the pork tenderloins and allow to marinate in the refrigerator for at least 1 hour, to a maximum of 3 hours.

Preheat grill to hottest setting.

Remove the pork from the marinade and season with salt and pepper to taste. Grill for 15 minutes, turning once, or to desired doneness. Remove from the grill and serve with peach salsa (page 180).

to serve

Place a grilled peach on each plate and top with a piece of grilled pork tenderloin. Spoon peach salsa over top and serve.

MAKES 6 SERVINGS

recipe continued on next page

Ingredients

9			**peaches (fully ripe)**
1 Tbsp.	·	15 mL	**olive oil**
1			**shallot, finely minced**
1 clove			**garlic, finely minced**
1 tsp.	·	5 mL	**chopped cilantro**
$\frac{1}{2}$			**jalapeño pepper, seeded and finely chopped**
1 tsp.	·	5 mL	**ginger, finely chopped**
3 Tbsp.	·	45 mL	**red onion, finely chopped**
2			**limes, juice of**
			kosher salt and white pepper to taste

Peach Salsa

Preheat grill to hottest setting.

Halve 3 of the peaches, and remove the stones. Drizzle with the olive oil. Place the peaches on the grill, cut-side down, and cook them until golden brown, but still slightly raw in the middle, about 10 minutes. Remove the peaches from the grill and keep warm.

Halve the remaining 6 peaches and remove the stones. Cube the raw peaches and combine with the remaining ingredients. Taste and adjust for seasoning. Let marinate at room temperature until ready to use.

Ingredients

6			**whole quail, deboned**
			kosher salt and white pepper to taste
3 sprigs			**thyme, finely chopped**
3 Tbsp.	·	30 mL	**olive oil**

Thyme Roasted Quail
with Garlic Sauce and Venturi-Schulze Balsamic Vinegar

This recipe encapsulates my vision of regional cuisine—artisanal foods brought together from across the country and harmonized on one plate. Venturi-Schulze balsamic vinegar is produced just outside of Victoria on Vancouver Island. It adds a tangy, smoky and caramel note to a perfectly roasted quail with notes of thyme and olive oil.

Season the quail with the salt and pepper, thyme and olive oil. Transfer to an ovenproof baking dish and refrigerate for 30 minutes.

Preheat oven to 375°F (190°C).

Place the quail in the oven and bake for 25 minutes or until cooked through. Leave the oven on.

to serve

½ lb.	·	250 g	**fresh baby greens**
3 Tbsp.	·	45 mL	**reduced Venturi-Schulze balsamic vinegar**
3 Tbsp.	·	45 mL	**Wild Rice Mimosa (page 182)**
pinch			**fleur de sel**

On each of 6 dinner plates, spoon 1 Tbsp. (15 mL) of the garlic sauce (page 182). Place a quail in each puddle of garlic sauce and drizzle with the reduced balsamic vinegar. Form quenelles with 2 Tbsp. (30 mL) of the wild rice mimosa and place beside the quail.

Sprinkle with fleur de sel and serve.

MAKES 6 SERVINGS

recipe continued on next page

Ingredients

½ cup	·	125 mL	**garlic cloves, peeled**
½ cup	·	125 mL	**olive oil**
1			**bay leaf**
1 sprig			**rosemary**
1 sprig			**thyme**
1 tsp.	·	5 mL	**black peppercorns**
3 Tbsp.	·	45 mL	**35% cream**
			kosher salt and white pepper to taste

Garlic Sauce

Combine all the ingredients, except the cream, in a small ovenproof saucepan and cover with a tight-fitting lid.

Place in the oven and bake for 35 minutes or until the garlic is very soft.

Using a slotted spoon, transfer the garlic from the oil into a blender. (Reserve the oil from the garlic confit for other uses.) Blend the garlic with the cream and return the sauce to a small saucepan.

Bring the garlic sauce to a simmer and season with salt and pepper to taste.

If the sauce seems too thick, loosen it up with a few teaspoonfuls of water.

Ingredients

2			**shallots, peeled and finely minced**
½			**clove garlic, peeled and finely minced**
½ cup	·	125 mL	**cooked wild rice**
½ cup	·	125 mL	**grated hard cooked eggs**
2 Tbsp.	·	30 mL	**mayonnaise (page 13)**
1			**lemon, juice of**
			kosher salt and white pepper to taste
2 Tbsp.	·	30 mL	**chives, minced**

Wild Rice Mimosa

Combine all the ingredients and refrigerate until required.

Ingredients

¼ cup	50 mL	**olive oil**
¼ cup	50 mL	**tomato ketchup**
¼ cup	50 mL	**dark brown sugar**
¼ cup	50 mL	**Gamay Noir**
2 Tbsp.	30 mL	**grape jelly**
2		**green onions (white part only), minced**
1 clove		**garlic, minced**
1 Tbsp.	15 mL	**ginger, finely minced**
1 Tbsp.	15 mL	**soy sauce**
2 tsp.	10 mL	**dried chili flakes**
1		**lemon, juice and zest of**
2 sprigs		**rosemary, chopped**
		kosher salt and white pepper to taste
6 lbs.	2.7 kg	**pork spareribs, cut into pieces**

Wine Country Spareribs

I love to barbecue. My parents never took vacations, but once or twice a summer they would drive down to the parks surrounding Niagara Falls. The main attraction was always the barbecue for lunch—always charcoal-fired and always with big chunks of mutton, veal and, my favorite, pork spareribs.

In a large bowl combine all the ingredients, except the spareribs, and whisk to incorporate. Place the ribs in the marinade, cover with plastic wrap and refrigerate overnight.

Preheat grill to moderate heat.

Remove the ribs from the marinade and pat dry with kitchen towel. Season with salt and pepper to taste and grill for 45 minutes, turning every so often to ensure equal coloring and cooking.

Remove the ribs from grill and serve. They taste especially good with homemade wine and bread.

MAKES 6 SERVINGS

Baked Vegetable
and Oka Cheese Pan Bread

*A delicious way to use up the
bounty of a summer harvest. Use
a variety of vegetables, such as
baby beans, asparagus, tomatoes,
whatever is in season. You could
also try a stronger cheese. This
cheese pan bread travels well and
is an ideal picnic food.*

Ingredients

2 Tbsp.	•	30 mL	**unsalted butter**
1 cup	•	250 mL	**mushrooms, quartered**
2 Tbsp.	•	30 mL	**olive oil**
1 cup	•	250 mL	**carrots, peeled, diced and blanched**
1			**zucchini, diced and blanched**
1½ cups	•	375 mL	**all-purpose flour**
1 tsp.	•	5 mL	**baking powder**
1 tsp.	•	5 mL	**celery salt**
1			**lemon, zest of, finely chopped**
6			**eggs**
1 cup	•	250 mL	**unsalted butter at room temperature**
½ cup	•	125 mL	**Oka cheese, rind removed, diced**
3			**green onions**
2 tsp.	•	10 mL	**garlic, chopped**
			kosher salt and white pepper to taste
2 Tbsp.	•	30 mL	**grated Parmesan cheese**

Melt the butter in a small sauté pan set over medium heat. Add the mushrooms and sauté until slightly browned, about 5 minutes, stirring frequently. Remove the mushrooms from the pan and set aside.

Preheat oven to 300°F (150°C).

In a bowl, combine the olive oil with the mushrooms, carrots and zucchini. Pour the vegetables onto an ovenproof dish and put the dish into the oven. Let the vegetables bake for 40 minutes then remove them from the oven and reserve.

In a bowl combine the flour, baking powder, celery salt and lemon zest. In the bowl of a stand mixer, add the eggs, one at a time, to the butter and whisk until smooth. Add the flour mixture to the butter mixture and mix until smooth. Mix in the vegetables and combine to form a pancake-like batter.

Add the Oka cheese, green onions and garlic. Season to taste with salt and pepper. Stir thoroughly to incorporate then set aside.

Preheat oven to 375°F (190°C).

Butter the insides of six 3-inch (7.5-cm) fry pans. Divide the vegetable-cheese mixture into each pan. Sprinkle the grated Parmesan over the batter. Bake for 40 minutes or until cooked through.

Turn out the cake and let it cool before slicing.

MAKES 6 SERVINGS

Ingredients

2 Tbsp. •	30 mL	**olive oil**
1		**onion, finely diced**
1		**stalk celery, peeled and finely diced**
1		**carrot, finely diced**
1 clove		**garlic, finely diced**
$\frac{1}{2}$ cup •	125 mL	**quinoa grain**
1 cup •	250 mL	**Chicken Stock (page 267) or water**

Duck Confit and Quinoa Tarts
with Sweet Onion Jam

Quinoa is my favorite ancient grain. First cultivated by the Incas of South America, it has been recognized as one of nature's perfect foods because it is rich in protein and amino acids. Quinoa has become a staple in many of the world's cuisines. It not only strengthens individual layers of flavor, but also adds an interesting texture.

In a small saucepot heat the olive oil over medium heat. Add the onion, celery, carrot and garlic and sauté for 5 minutes, stirring frequently. Add the quinoa and stock or water and bring to a boil. Reduce the heat and simmer for 10 minutes. Using a fine colander, strain the quinoa and let cool to room temperature. Discard the liquid and refrigerate the cooked quinoa until required.

MAKES 6 SERVINGS
recipe continued on next page

Ingredients

6			unbaked tart shells (see Basic Pie Dough, below)
½ cup	•	125 mL	cooked quinoa
½ cup	•	125 mL	Duck Confit (page 34), roughly chopped
½ cup	•	125 mL	soft goat cheese
6 Tbsp.	•	90 mL	Sweet Onion Jam (page 190)
2 Tbsp.	•	30 mL	olive oil
6 sprigs			chervil

to assemble the duck tarts

Preheat oven to 425°F (220°C).

Line 6 tart shells with the pie dough and bake blind until golden brown, about 12–15 minutes.

Combine the cooked quinoa with the duck confit and spoon into the tart shells. Spread a generous amount of goat cheese over the quinoa mixture and smooth the top. Place a dollop of sweet onion jam on top and drizzle with the olive oil. Garnish with a sprig of chervil and serve.

Ingredients

3 cups	•	750 mL	all-purpose flour
1 tsp.	•	5 mL	salt
1 cup	•	250 mL	cold butter cut into small cubes
2 large			egg yolks
¼ cup	•	50 mL	ice water

Basic Pie Dough

Combine the flour with the salt and add the butter. Using a knife or pastry blender, cut the pastry/butter mix until it resembles coarse meal. Add the egg yolks and ice water until a firm ball is formed. Do not overwork the dough. Wrap in plastic and chill for 30 minutes before using.

Ingredients

2 Tbsp. •	30 mL	**olive oil**
2 Tbsp. •	30 mL	**unsalted butter**
2 cups •	500 mL	**onions, thinly sliced**
1 clove		**garlic, thinly sliced**
½ cup •	125 mL	**Gamay Noir**
2 Tbsp. •	30 mL	**brown sugar**
1 Tbsp. •	15 mL	**red wine vinegar**

Sweet Onion Jam

In a sauté pan set over medium heat, heat the olive oil and the butter until the butter is frothy. Add the onions, reduce heat to low and stir frequently for about 5 minutes or until the onions are golden brown. Add the garlic and continue cooking for 2 minutes, stirring.

Add the Gamay Noir, brown sugar and vinegar and bring to a boil. Reduce the heat and simmer until the liquid has evaporated and the onion mixture is thick. Remove from the heat and let cool to room temperature. Reserve until required.

Ingredients

2 lbs. • 1 kg	**sweetbreads**
1	**onion, chopped**
1	**carrot, chopped**
2 stalks	**celery, chopped**
2 cloves	**garlic, chopped**
2	**tomatoes, seeded and chopped**
2	**bay leaves**
2 sprigs	**thyme**
1 sprig	**rosemary**
2 cups • 500 mL	**white wine**
3 cups • 750 mL	**cold water**

Pan-Seared Sweetbreads
in Clover Honey with Apple Tomato Chutney

Clover honey can be found in many health food stores. It gives this recipe a wonderful layer of flavor that is lacking in regular honey. Sweetbreads are gaining in popularity for their subtle flavor and magnificent texture.

Combine all the ingredients in a large soup pot and bring to a boil. Reduce the heat and simmer the sweetbreads for 1 hour. Remove the pot from the heat and let the contents cool to room temperature. When the sweetbreads are cool enough to handle, peel off the outer membrane. Discard the membranes and refrigerate the sweetbreads in marinade (page 194).

to serve

Remove the sweetbreads from the marinade and pat dry. In a large sauté pan set over medium-high heat melt 2 Tbsp. (30 mL) butter. When the butter is frothy, add the sweetbreads and cook to golden brown, about 3 minutes per side. Remove the sweetbreads and keep them warm.

Serve sweetbreads on warmed plates with a generous spoonful of the chutney (see page 195).

MAKES 6 SERVINGS

recipe continued on the next three pages

Ingredients

¼ cup	• 50 mL	**clover honey**
¼ cup	• 50 mL	**olive oil**
¼ cup	• 50 mL	**Gamay Noir**
1 Tbsp.	• 15 mL	**thyme, finely chopped**
1 tsp.	• 5 mL	**crushed black pepper**
1 tsp.	• 5 mL	**crushed coriander seeds**

for the sweetbread marinade

Combine all the ingredients in a large bowl and add the sweet-breads. Marinate in the refrigerator for 1 hour.

Ingredients

¹⁄₄ cup	·	50 mL	**vegetable oil**
1			**onion, finely chopped**
1			**red pepper, seeded and finely chopped**
2 cloves			**garlic, finely chopped**
1 tsp.	·	5 mL	**ground allspice**
1 tsp.	·	5 mL	**mustard seeds**
2 tsp.	·	10 mL	**cracked black pepper**
1 Tbsp.	·	15 mL	**grated ginger**
1			**bay leaf**
2 lbs.	·	1 kg	**apples, peeled, cored and chopped**
1 lb.	·	500 g	**tomatoes, peeled, seeded and chopped**
¹⁄₂ cup	·	125 mL	**white wine vinegar**
			water as needed
¹⁄₄ cup	·	50 mL	**brown sugar**
¹⁄₂ cup	·	125 mL	**sultanas (or raisins) soaked in warm water**
1 tsp.	·	5 mL	**chili flakes**

Apple Tomato Chutney

Using a large stockpot set over medium-high heat, add the olive oil and the onions. Sauté the onions for 5 minutes without allowing them to color. Add the red pepper and garlic. Stirring frequently to prevent the vegetables from coloring, add the allspice, mustard seeds, black pepper, ginger and bay leaf. Stir to combine and reduce the heat to medium.

Add the apples and tomatoes and stir to combine with the onions and spices

Let the tomatoes and apples cook for 15 minutes, stirring frequently so they don't brown. Add the white wine vinegar and just enough water to cover the contents of the pot (about 2 cups/ 500 mL). Allow the chutney to come to a slow simmer, stirring frequently. When the liquid has evaporated and the chutney has thickened (35–45 minutes), remove the sultanas from the warm water and squeeze them dry. Stir the sultanas, brown sugar and chili flakes into the chutney. Remove from the heat and let cool to room temperature.

Ingredients

½ cup	125 mL	**cannellini beans (white navy beans)**
3 cups	750 mL	**water**
¼ cup	50 mL	**olive oil**
2		**red onions, chopped**
3 cloves		**garlic, finely chopped**
1		**carrot, peeled and finely chopped**
1		**leek (white part only), finely chopped**
1 stalk		**celery, peeled and finely chopped**
2		**tomatoes, seeded and finely chopped**
3 oz.	90 g	**prosciutto, finely diced**
2 tsp.	10 mL	**tomato paste**
4 cups	1 L	**water**
1 Tbsp.	15 mL	**rosemary, finely chopped**
1 Tbsp.	15 mL	**thyme, finely chopped**
		kosher salt and white pepper to taste

Divinely Inspired White Bean Soup

In October 2003, I was invited by Nicolette Novak of the Good Earth Cooking School to join a culinary tour of Tuscany, Italy. The highlight of the trip was when I went south to my home town of Avellino. I stayed a few nights with my aunt who is a nun and runs a school not far from the house I was born in. I was invited to dine with the nuns of the school and this soup was what was they served. It proved to be such a memorable experience that I donated my traveling chef knife collection to the school and they assured me I would be blessed by such a selfless act!

Cover the beans with 3 cups (750 mL) of cold water and soak at room temperature overnight. Drain the beans through a colander and reserve until required. In a heavy pot set over moderate heat, heat the olive oil and sauté the onions and garlic for 2 minutes.

Add the carrot, leek, celery, tomatoes and prosciutto, and sauté for 2 minutes or until the vegetables have browned slightly. Stir in the tomato paste, then the beans. Bring to a boil in the 4 cups (1 L) of water then reduce the heat and simmer for 1 hour or until the beans have cooked through and are soft.

Purée the soup in a food processor or blender, then return it to the soup pot. Bring back to a simmer, add the chopped herbs and serve.

MAKES 6 SERVINGS

Ingredients

2 Tbsp. •	30 mL	**olive oil**
2 Tbsp. •	30 mL	**unsalted butter**
1 tsp. •	5 mL	**ground cumin seed**
1 tsp. •	5 mL	**ground ginger**
1 tsp. •	5 mL	**ground coriander seed**
1/2 cup •	125 mL	**onion, finely diced**
1/2 cup •	125 mL	**celery, peeled and finely diced**
1/2 cup •	125 mL	**carrot, peeled and finely diced**
2 Tbsp. •	30 mL	**garlic, finely minced**
1 cup •	250 mL	**green lentils, rinsed in cold water and drained**
4 cups •	1 L	**Chicken Stock (page 267)**
		kosher salt and white pepper to taste

Green Lentil Tapenade
with Cumin-Scented Sour Cream

Slowly simmered lentils are the perfect winter taste for me. Served warm with a drizzle of olive oil and aged balsamic vinegar, lentils make a nice accompaniment to full-flavored winter foods such as pheasant, quail and capon. When puréed, lentils make a delicious spread, ideal for slathering on warm country bread or as a garnish to a thick winter soup.

In a medium stockpot, heat the olive oil to moderately high and add the butter.

When the butter is frothy, add the cumin, ginger and coriander. Stir with a wooden spoon, being careful not to burn the spices.

When the spices have released their aroma, after about 30 seconds, add the onion, celery and carrot. Sauté for 5 minutes until all the vegetables are coated with the spices and have softened. Add the garlic and stir for 3–5 minutes. Stir in the lentils and the chicken stock and bring to a boil. Reduce the heat and simmer for 45 minutes to an hour. Remove from the heat and let cool to room temperature or until the lentils have become soft enough to squish between your fingers.

Sieve the cooked lentils to separate them from the stock, reserving both. Purée the lentils in a food processor. Add some of the reserved stock to loosen the lentil purée and season with salt and pepper to taste.

MAKES 2 CUPS/500 ML

Ingredients

½ tsp.	•	2.5 mL	**cumin seed, finely ground to a powder**
½ cup	•	125 mL	**sour cream**
1 Tbsp.	•	15 mL	**dill, finely chopped**
1			**lemon, juice of**

Cumin-Scented Sour Cream

Combine all the ingredients and fold into the lentil purée.
Keep refrigerated until ready to serve.

Ingredients

1			**bulb garlic, cloves peeled and sliced paper thin**
1 cup	•	250 mL	**vegetable oil**
			kosher salt to taste

Garlic Chips

Heat the oil to 360°F (185°C).

Fry the thinly sliced garlic until golden brown, about 2 minutes,

Using a slotted spoon, carefully remove the garlic onto a plate
lined with kitchen towel to absorb excess oil. Season the
chips with salt and use as a garnish.

Ingredients

2 cups	•	500 mL	white wine
3/4 cup	•	175 mL	light corn syrup
3/4 cup	•	175 mL	dark corn syrup
1/4 cup	•	50 mL	soy sauce
2 Tbsp.	•	30 mL	coriander, finely chopped
4			star anise
3			duck breasts, approx. 1/2 lb. (250 g) each

Roasted Duck
with Sweet and Sour Sauce

This recipe was inspired by a trip in 2002 to Beijing, China where I was invited by the hotel Kempinski to prepare Canadian-themed meals for a week. I was fascinated by the preparation of the Peking duck and the secrecy involved. This recipe was inspired by my Chinese memories.

In a container large enough to hold the duck in a single layer, whisk the wine with the corn syrups and the soy sauce until well incorporated. Add the coriander and the star anise. Place the duck in the marinade, cover and refrigerate for 24 hours.

Preheat oven to 450°F (230°C). Remove the duck from the marinade and pat dry. Reserve the marinade. Place the duck skin-side down in a roasting pan and place in the oven. Cook the duck to an internal temperature of 140°F (65°C) for about 15–20 minutes.

MAKES 6 SERVINGS
recipe continued on next page

Ingredients

2		**limes, juice and julienned zest of**
1 Tbsp. •	15 mL	**ginger, finely chopped**
2 cups •	500 mL	**water**
$^1/_4$ cup •	50 mL	**granulated sugar**
$^3/_4$ cup •	175 mL	**Chicken Stock (page 267)**

Sweet and Sour Sauce

Combine the lime zest, juice, ginger, water and sugar in a
small saucepot and bring to a gentle boil. Reduce the heat and
simmer for 30 minutes. Strain the lime and ginger mixture
and add to the chicken stock. Bring the stock to a simmer and
reduce by half.

Bring $^1/_2$ cup (125 mL) of the reserved marinade to a boil in a
small saucepan. Reduce the heat and simmer gently until
reduced by half. Add the reserved lime and ginger stock and
bring mixture to a boil. Reduce the heat and simmer until the
sauce thickens. Strain the sauce through a sieve and keep
warm.

Let the duck rest out of the oven for 5 minutes, then slice it
thinly and serve with sweet and sour sauce spooned over top.

Ingredients

¹⁄₂ cup	· 125 mL	**extra virgin olive oil**
		kosher salt and white pepper to taste
2 sprigs		**thyme, finely chopped**
1 sprig		**rosemary, finely chopped**
1 Tbsp.	· 15 mL	**Dijon mustard**
1		**lemon, zest of**
2 cloves		**garlic, finely chopped**
6		**capon breasts, wing bone on and skin intact**
6 Tbsp.	· 90 mL	**black truffle paste**

Truffle Roasted Capon
with Gamay Noir Mushroom Sauce

Capon is the meat of a young rooster, usually brought to market by the time it's 10 months old. The special corn diet the roosters are fed yields plump juicy meat that is perfectly suited to roasting. For this recipe use whatever mushrooms are in season in your area.

Place the olive oil in a bowl with the salt and pepper, thyme, rosemary, Dijon mustard, lemon zest and garlic. Add the capons, cover with plastic wrap and refrigerate for 3 hours. Remove the capon from the marinade and pat dry. Discard the marinade.

Preheat oven to 350°F (180°C).

Place the capon on a clean work surface and gently lift the skin with your fingers. Place 1 Tbsp. (15 mL) of black truffle paste under the skin of each capon breast. Place the capon on a baking tray skin-side up and roast for 40 minutes or until a meat thermometer reads 160°F (75°C). Remove the capons from the oven and let them rest.

MAKES 6 SERVINGS

recipe continued on next page

Ingredients

¼ cup	• 50 mL	**olive oil**
2 Tbsp.	• 30 mL	**unsalted butter**
2		**shallots, finely chopped**
1 clove		**garlic, finely chopped**
2 cups	• 500 mL	**wild mushrooms, roughly chopped**
1 cup	• 250 mL	**Gamay Noir**
¼ cup	• 50 mL	**Chicken Stock (page 267)**
½ cup	• 125 mL	**tomatoes, cored, seeded and diced**
¼ cup	• 50 mL	**35% cream**
1		**lemon, juice of**
		kosher salt and white pepper to taste
1 Tbsp.	• 15 mL	**chives, finely minced**

Gamay Noir Mushroom Sauce

In a large sauté pan heat the olive oil over medium-high heat and add the butter. When the butter is frothy, add the shallots and garlic. Cook for a few minutes, stirring frequently to avoid any coloring, then add the mushrooms and the Gamay Noir. Bring to a boil and simmer for about 25 minutes, until only ½ cup (125 mL) remains in the pan.

Add the chicken stock, tomatoes and cream. Bring to a boil and simmer until the mushroom tomato sauce has reduced by half and thickened. Add the lemon juice and adjust the seasoning to taste.

Remove the sauce from the heat and divide between 6 large dinner plates. Place the capons on top of the sauce.

Spring

Merlot Mushroom Soup

Veal Medallions
with Grilled Asparagus,
Aged Cheddar and Morels

Rosemary Chicken Breast
with Chanterelles and
Polenta Frites

Eggs Poached in Merlot
with Bacon

Summer

Braised Bison Ribs
with Horseradish Mashed Potatoes

Roasted Duck Breast
with Quinoa and Cherry Merlot Reduction

Sea Scallops
with Foie Gras and Red Wine Risotto

Merlot

WORKING AT HILLEBRAND ESTATES WINERY HAS AFFORDED ME the great privilege of working with some very talented and special people who have mentored me and provided me with the foundation and confidence needed to do my work. One such person was our wine maker J.L. Groux, who has been a wonderful resource for me in my quest to create an identifiable Canadian wine country cuisine. I have been very fortunate and you can imagine how much the other chefs would love to have access to their own personal wine maker.

One of my favorite wines that J.L. has produced was the 1998 Showcase Cabernet Merlot. Merlot is the grape so famously crafted into the famous Pétrus, St. Emilion and Pomerol wines. At Hillebrand Estates, Merlot is one of the three wines used to make our own famous

Autumn

Braised Lamb Shanks
with Penne and Asiago

Wild Mushroom Polenta
with Tomato Sauce

Caribou Osso Buco

Winter

Orecchiette
with Pheasant, Swiss Chard
and Blue Cheese

Icewine Elk Tenderloin
with Chanterelles and Red Currants

Beef and Sage Medallions
with Sweet Potato Chips

label Trius Red. Trius Red is a classic Bordeaux blend including Cabernet Franc and Cabernet Sauvignon. Merlot is the grape that contributes softness, suppleness and generally rounds out the flavor.

Merlot's flavor profile can be very broad but generally it features easily accessible fruit such as currants, black cherries and plums. It can add notes of bay leaf, clove and green peppercorns. Older wines may also contribute flavors of mushrooms and truffles, vanilla, cedar and coffee. In France, where this grape originates, it is one of the most widely planted grapes. However, in the New World it generally takes on a leading role. With the possible exceptions of the labels I mentioned above, Merlot in France is a blended wine. It is a best supporting actor as opposed to the leading man. Whether it is because the word is easy to spell and pronounce (compared to other French varietals), or because it is a softer, less tannic and more approachable wine, Merlot is a red wine for red wine drinkers (as opposed to red wine collectors).

I have enjoyed and would recommend Merlot for any season. On the patio enjoying Braised Bison Ribs, or during the winter with Beef and Sage Medallions, Merlot is suited to many recipes. It is a staple in any well-stocked wine country kitchen.

Ingredients

2 Tbsp.	•	30 mL	**olive oil**
2 Tbsp.	•	30 mL	**unsalted butter**
1			**onion, finely chopped**
½ cup	•	125 mL	**celery, finely chopped**
½ cup	•	125 mL	**leeks, finely chopped**
2 tsp.	•	10 mL	**garlic, finely chopped**
6 cups	•	1.5 L	**assorted mushrooms**
1 cup	•	250 mL	**Merlot**
1 cup	•	250 mL	**Chicken Stock (page 267)**
1 cup	•	250 mL	**35% cream**
			kosher salt and white pepper to taste
2 tsp.	•	10 mL	**lemon juice**
2 Tbsp.	•	30 mL	**Italian parsley, chopped**
1 Tbsp.	•	15 mL	**chives, finely chopped**
½ cup	•	125 mL	**35% cream, whipped to stiff peaks**

Merlot Mushroom Soup

The original version of this soup was created at the Windsor Arms Hotel. When I came to Hillebrand Estates Winery Restaurant, I created this variation based on Merlot. The addition of the red wine gives an added dimension of flavor that tastes of wine country. If you have access to seasonal wild mushrooms, be sure to include them for texture and flavor.

In a medium soup pot over moderate heat, warm the olive oil and the butter. When the butter is frothy add the onion, celery, leeks and garlic. When the vegetables have softened, after about 5 minutes, add the mushrooms and continue cooking until the mushrooms have wilted slightly. Add the Merlot and chicken stock. Increase the heat to high and bring to a boil.

Reduce the heat to a simmer and cook until the mushrooms have cooked through, about 15 minutes. Add the 1 cup (250 mL) of 35% cream and continue to simmer for 15 minutes. Transfer the soup to a blender or food processor and blend until smooth.

Return the soup to the heat and bring to a boil. Add the lemon juice, salt and pepper and herbs.

Ladle the soup into warm bowls and top with a generous dollop of whipped cream.

MAKES 6 SERVINGS

Ingredients

2 lbs.	•	1 kg	**veal tenderloin, divided into 6 portions**
2 Tbsp.	•	30 mL	**olive oil**
			kosher salt and white pepper to taste
1 Tbsp.	•	15 mL	**tarragon, finely chopped**
2 tsp.	•	10 mL	**Italian parsley, chopped**
1 Tbsp.	•	15 mL	**thyme, chopped**
2 Tbsp.	•	30 mL	**unsalted butter**
1 Tbsp.	•	15 mL	**olive oil**
60 spears			**fresh asparagus, blanched**
6 slices			**extra aged cheddar**

Veal Medallions
with Grilled Asparagus, Aged Cheddar and Morels

The marriage of asparagus and morel mushrooms is not new to gastronomy. I brought the two together here with a luscious aged cheddar sauce to showcase the affinity of Merlot to aged, hard cheese. I have been making this recipe every May for over 10 years and it has become a favorite during mother's day celebrations.

Preheat oven to 450°F (230°C). Preheat grill to high, 500°F (260°C).

Place the veal in a bowl and add 2 Tbsp. (30 mL) olive oil, salt and pepper, tarragon, parsley and thyme. Set aside.

In a large ovenproof sauté pan set over medium-high heat melt the butter. When the butter is frothy, add the veal. Immediately transfer the sauté pan to the oven. Cook for 10 minutes, then turn the meat and continue cooking for 5 minutes. Remove from the oven and keep the veal warm.

Meanwhile, toss the asparagus with 1 Tbsp. (15 mL) of olive oil and grill for 3 minutes or until the asparagus has charred nicely. Place the asparagus spears on the veal. Keep warm until required.

MAKES 6 SERVINGS

recipe continued on next page

Ingredients

2 Tbsp. · 30 mL		**unsalted butter**
1		**shallot, finely minced**
1/4 cup · 50 mL		**asparagus trimming (not peel)**
1 clove		**garlic, finely chopped**
1/2 cup · 125 mL		**white wine**
1/4 cup · 50 mL		**veal stock**
2 Tbsp. · 30 mL		**35% cream**
2 Tbsp. · 30 mL		**unsalted butter**
1 tsp. · 5 mL		**lemon juice**
6 sprigs		**tarragon**
		kosher salt and white pepper to taste
2 Tbsp. · 30 mL		**diced roasted peppers for garnish**

for the cream

Heat the 2 Tbsp. (30 mL) butter in a small saucepan set over medium heat. When the butter is frothy, add the shallot, asparagus trimmings and garlic. Sauté for 2 minutes, stirring frequently. Add the white wine and the veal stock.

Bring to a boil, reduce the heat and simmer until only 1/4 cup (50 mL) of liquid remains.

Add the cream and simmer until reduced by half. Strain the sauce through a sieve into another small saucepan and add the remaining butter. Bring to a simmer and add the lemon juice, tarragon and salt and pepper to taste. Keep the sauce warm until required.

Ingredients

2 cups · 500 mL		**morel mushrooms**
1/4 cup · 50 mL		**Chicken Stock (page 267)**
		kosher salt and white pepper to taste
2 tsp · 10 mL		**chives, finely chopped**
1 tsp. · 5 mL		**tarragon, finely chopped**
1 tsp. · 5 mL		**lemon juice**

for the morels

Combine the mushrooms and the chicken stock in a small pot and bring to a rapid boil. Reduce the heat and simmer until the mushrooms have wilted. Strain the mushrooms, reserving the liquid for another use. Put the mushrooms in a small bowl and season with salt and pepper, chives, tarragon and lemon juice. Reserve until required.

to serve

Place a puddle of aged cheddar sauce on each plate. Place a
piece of veal on top of the sauce and top with the grilled
asparagus. Sprinkle the mushrooms around the veal and
garnish with the diced peppers and more of the aged cheese.

Ingredients

6		**chicken breasts, with skin intact and wing bone on**
6 sprigs		**rosemary, leaves picked off**
2 Tbsp. ·	30 mL	**olive oil**
		kosher salt and white pepper to taste

Rosemary Chicken Breast
with Chanterelles and Polenta Frites

When I was working in Germany, an opportunity to forage for mushrooms was nearly overshadowed by the fact that, owing to my nearsightednes, I trampled over hundreds of dollars' worth of these mushrooms by accident. It was only because I was tackled by a colleague that we were able to bring any back to the restaurant. Apparently they were yelling at me to be careful, but as I couldn't understand German at the time, I took the yelling for youthful exuberance.

Preheat oven to 375°F (190°C).

Gently lift the skin off the chicken breasts. Insert a sprig of rosemary under the skin of each breast. Sprinkle the chicken with the olive oil and salt and pepper.

Place on a baking tray, skin-side down, and roast for 12–15 minutes or until a meat thermometer registers 160°F (75°C). Remove from the oven and keep warm.

MAKES 6 SERVINGS

Ingredients

2 Tbsp. ·	30 mL	**olive oil**
2 Tbsp. ·	30 mL	**unsalted butter**
2		**shallots, finely chopped**
1 clove		**garlic, finely chopped**
3 cups ·	750 mL	**chanterelle mushrooms, halved**
		kosher salt and white pepper to taste
½ cup ·	125 mL	**white wine**
½ cup ·	125 mL	**Chicken Stock (page 267)**
2 Tbsp. ·	30 mL	**champagne vinegar**

for the chanterelle stew

In a large sauté pan set over medium-high heat warm the olive oil and the butter. When the butter is frothy add the shallots and the garlic. Stir for 2 minutes then add the chanterelles. Stir frequently for 15 minutes then add the white wine and boil it down until very little liquid is left. Add the stock and the vinegar and season with salt and pepper. Remove from the heat and reserve.

Ingredients

1 cup	• 250 mL	**water**
1 cup	• 250 mL	**whole milk**
		kosher salt and white pepper to taste
1½ cups	• 375 mL	**cornmeal**
1 Tbsp.	• 15 mL	**rosemary, chopped**
1 Tbsp.	• 15 mL	**sage, chopped**
½ cup	• 125 mL	**grated Parmesan cheese**
½ tsp.	• 2 mL	**chili paste**
2 Tbsp.	• 30 mL	**unsalted butter**
4 cups	• 1 L	**vegetable oil for deep frying**

Polenta Frites

This makes more than you will need for one meal, but it can be stored in the freezer, tightly wrapped, for 3 months.

Bring the water and milk to a rapid boil in a medium-sized saucepan and add salt and pepper (taste the water, it should taste slightly salty). Add the cornmeal in a steady stream, stirring constantly with a wooden spoon. Add the herbs, cheese, chili paste and butter. Simmer, stirring often, until the polenta pulls away from the sides of the pan, about 30 minutes. Pour the polenta into a shallow casserole dish, smooth the surface and refrigerate for 2 hours.

Preheat the vegetable oil in a large deep fryer to 360°F (185°C).

When thoroughly chilled and set, remove the polenta from the refrigerator and turn out of the casserole onto a cutting surface. Slice the polenta into finger-sized frites. Gently submerge the polenta frites into the hot oil and deep fry until golden brown, about 3 minutes. Sprinkle the frites with salt and serve with the chicken and mushroom stew.

Ingredients

2 Tbsp.	· 30 mL	**unsalted butter**
1/3 cup	· 75 mL	**1-inch (2-cm) strips smoked bacon**
1		**shallot, finely chopped**
3 cups	· 750 mL	**spinach, washed and stems removed**
2 cups	· 500 mL	**Merlot**
8		**eggs**
6 cups	· 1.5 L	**assorted spring lettuces**

Eggs Poached in Merlot with Bacon

This fun recipe comes from an idea I had after reading that in some wine regions of France, eggs are poached in the lees of wine. I particularly enjoy eating these eggs soft so the egg yolks mingle with the wine-colored egg white to create a wonderful purple hue. This versatile recipe can be prepared with other spring greens or watercress.

In a medium saucepan, melt 1 Tbsp. (15 mL) butter over medium heat. Add the smoked bacon and continue cooking, stirring frequently until the bacon is crisp. Remove the bacon to a plate lined with kitchen towel, and keep it warm.

Pour out some of the bacon grease and add the remaining butter to the pan. When the butter melts, add the shallots and spinach, stirring frequently until the spinach wilts. Remove the spinach and keep it warm.

Add the wine to the pan. Bring the wine to a boil then reduce the heat to a gentle simmer.

Crack the eggs into the simmering red wine, one at a time, and poach to desired doneness, about 2–5 minutes.

In a small mixing bowl combine the cooked bacon and the spinach and season with salt and pepper. Divide the mixture among 4 plates, top with poached eggs and serve.

MAKES 4 SERVINGS

Ingredients

1 cup	·	250 mL	**olive oil (or more as needed)**
3 cups	·	750 mL	**all-purpose flour**
			kosher salt and white pepper to taste
1 Tbsp.	·	15 mL	**cayenne pepper**
2 tsp.	·	10 mL	**sweet paprika**
1 Tbsp.	·	15 mL	**rosemary, chopped**
1 Tbsp.	·	15 mL	**thyme, chopped**
18			**bison ribs cut into individual pieces**

Braised Bison Ribs
with Horseradish Mashed Potatoes

This recipe defines comfort food. It was created by my sous chef, Ross Midgley, during the winter of 2002. Bison meat is increasingly easy to find in local markets and I recommend it as an elegant alternative to beef. Bison is dense, rich meat that pairs well with Merlot.

Heat the olive oil in a large ovenproof sauté pan (with a lid) set over high heat.

In the meantime, combine the flour with the salt and pepper, cayenne pepper, paprika, rosemary and thyme. Dredge the ribs in the flour until well coated. Place the ribs, one at a time, into the hot oil and brown them on both sides, about 3 minutes per side. Remove the browned ribs, discard any oil left in the pan and reserve the pan.

MAKES 6 SERVINGS

Ingredients

4 oz.	·	125 g	**unsalted butter**
½ cup	·	125 mL	**onion, chopped**
½ cup	·	125 mL	**carrot, chopped**
½ cup	·	125 mL	**celery, chopped**
1			**red pepper, seeded and chopped**
1			**fennel bulb, chopped**
4 cloves			**garlic, chopped**
1 Tbsp.	·	15 mL	**star anise**
1 Tbsp.	·	15 mL	**coriander seed**
1 Tbsp.	·	15 mL	**mustard seed**
2 tsp.	·	10 mL	**juniper berries**
1 pod			**vanilla bean, split**
5			**bay leaves**
18			**cooked bison ribs**
3 cups	·	750 mL	**fresh blueberries**
1 cup	·	250 mL	**molasses**
1 cup	·	250 mL	**plum tomatoes, chopped and liquid discarded**
1 cup	·	250 mL	**red wine**
8 cups	·	2 L	**Chicken Stock (page 267)**
			water as needed

for the braise

Preheat oven to 400°F (200°C).

Melt the butter in the pan used to sear the bison ribs. When the butter is frothy, add the onion, carrot, celery, red pepper, fennel and garlic. Stir frequently as the vegetables sauté and become lightly browned, about 10 minutes. Season with the 6 spices. Add the bison ribs and cover with the fresh blueberries, molasses, tomatoes, wine and stock. Bring to a boil, reduce the heat to a simmer. Add water as necessary to cover the ribs completely and cover with a tight-fitting lid.

Place into the preheated oven and braise until ribs are fork tender (3–4 hours depending on your stove, the meat should be just falling off the bone).

Carefully remove from the oven and let cool for approximately 15 minutes. Remove the ribs carefully from the pot (use kitchen tongs) and serve with the horseradish mashed potatoes (page 218).

recipe continued on next page

Ingredients

6		**large Yukon gold potatoes, well scrubbed**
$\frac{1}{2}$ cup	· 125 mL	**milk**
2 oz.	· 60 g	**unsalted butter**
1 Tbsp.	· 15 mL	**prepared horseradish**
1 Tbsp.	· 15 mL	**chives, finely chopped**

Horseradish Mashed Potatoes

Preheat oven to 400°F (200°C).

Cover potatoes with aluminum foil and pierce with the end of a sharp knife.

Bake for 1 hour or until they are cooked through. Remove from the oven and when cool remove the aluminum foil and scoop the flesh into a bowl.

Combine the milk and butter in a small saucepan and heat until the butter melts. Pour the butter mixture into the potatoes and mash until combined but not smooth. Add the horseradish and chives.

Serve with the braised bison ribs.

Roasted Duck Breast
with Quinoa and Cherry Merlot Reduction

This recipe was created for our feature story in The Buffalo News *in 1997. It was probably my first successful attempt at echoing the flavors found on the plate with those found in the glass. For example, the taste of cherries is a common flavor in Merlot. I therefore added Merlot to a duck stock reduction and used cherries to ensure the flavor of the dish was also predominately cherry.*

Ingredients

3   **whole duck breasts,
              each weighing 6 oz./175 g**

            kosher salt and white pepper to taste

Preheat the oven to 400˚F (200˚C).

Season the duck breasts, place them on a non-stick baking sheet and bake, skin-side down, for 35 minutes. Do not turn the duck breasts while baking. Remove from the oven and let the meat rest for 5 minutes.

Carve the duck and place equal portions on 6 warm dinner plates. Serve accompanied by quinoa salad and cherry sauce.

MAKES 6 SERVINGS
recipe continued on next page

Ingredients

1 cup	·	250 mL	**duck stock**
1 cup	·	250 mL	**quinoa, rinsed in cold water and strained**
			kosher salt and white pepper to taste
$\frac{1}{2}$ tsp.	·	2 mL	**orange oil**
1			**shallot, finely chopped**
2 Tbsp.	·	30 mL	**olive oil**
1 Tbsp.	·	15 mL	**sherry wine vinegar**

for the quinoa salad

In a small saucepan over medium-high heat bring the duck stock to a simmer. Pour the quinoa into the simmering stock and cook for about 25 minutes or until the duck stock has been absorbed. Add the remaining ingredients and season with salt and pepper.

Ingredients

1 cup	·	250 mL	**veal stock**
1 cup	·	250 mL	**Merlot**
1 cup	·	250 mL	**sweet cherries**
1 Tbsp.	·	15 mL	**unsalted butter**
2 Tbsp.	·	30 mL	**honey**
1 Tbsp.	·	15 mL	**sherry vinegar**

for the wine sauce

In a small saucepan reduce the veal stock until only $\frac{1}{4}$ cup (50 mL) remains. Add the Merlot, bring to a boil and reduce again until only $\frac{1}{2}$ cup (125 mL) remains.

Add the cherries, butter, honey and sherry vinegar. Bring to a boil, reduce heat and simmer until the cherries have cooked down and the sauce has thickened slightly, about 10 minutes. Keep sauce warm.

*I have been asked many times
what my "specialty" is. I have
never been able to give a clear
answer; mostly I just mumble
and hope for a laugh. It is only
since I have been with Hillebrand*

Sea Scallops
with Foie Gras and Red Wine Risotto

*Estates that I have discovered my
true culinary soul. This recipe is
a reflection of that soul. It is the
closest I feel I have ever come to
realizing a completely original
wine country recipe. To me, this
is wine country. A perfect blend
of great taste, beautiful appearance, delicate nuances and a
vague line between where the
food stops and the wine begins.*

Ingredients

6			**sea scallops**
			kosher salt and white pepper to taste
6 oz.	•	175 g	**foie gras, divided into 6 portions**
2 Tbsp.	•	30 mL	**olive oil**

Season the scallops with salt and pepper.

Place a large sauté pan over high heat. Season the foie gras
with salt and pepper and add to the hot pan. Sear the foie gras
until golden brown on each side, about 1 minute per side.

Remove from the heat and transfer to a plate with kitchen
towels to absorb excess fat.

Pour the excess fat out of the sauté pan and return the pan
to high heat. Add the scallops and cook on one side only until
crispy brown, about 2 minutes. Remove from the heat and
keep warm.

MAKES 6 SERVINGS

recipe continued on next page

Ingredients

2 cups	•	500 mL	**Merlot**
4 cups	•	1 L	**Chicken Stock (page 267)**
2 Tbsp.	•	30 mL	**unsalted butter**
2			**shallots, finely chopped**
1 tsp.	•	5 mL	**garlic, minced**
1 cup	•	250 mL	**Arborio short grain rice**
1 cup	•	250 mL	**fava beans, peeled and blanched**
2 Tbsp.	•	30 mL	**grated Parmesan cheese**
			kosher salt and white pepper to taste

Red Wine Risotto

Place the Merlot in a small saucepan over medium heat and reduce until only 2 Tbsp. (30 mL) of wine remains and has a syrupy consistency. Reserve.

Bring the chicken stock to a rapid boil.

In a large sauté pan set over medium heat, melt the butter with the shallots. Sauté the shallots until soft, stirring frequently, for about 5 minutes. Add the garlic, stir for 2 minutes, then stir in the Arborio rice.

Using a small ladle, transfer the boiling chicken stock to the rice. Stir with a wooden spoon until all of the stock has been absorbed. Continue to stir for 18–20 minutes, or until the rice is just cooked through and creamy.

Remove from the heat and fold in the fava beans, Parmesan and salt and pepper. Using a rubber spatula, scrape the red wine reduction into the risotto. Stir to blend well.

Divide the risotto among 6 warm dinner plates and top with the seared scallops. Place a piece of seared foie gras on each scallop and serve.

Braised Lamb Shanks
with Penne and Asiago

Braised lamb shanks are a staple on our fall and winter menus. I love the whole process involved in cooking this delicious meat. Lamb shank comes from the leg of lamb and is a tougher meat, but slow cooking and a little bit of love will render it melt-in-your-mouth tender. It takes hours to cook lamb shank; it must be on low heat and it must be well seasoned to reveal its inherent beauty. The result is a very satisfying winter meal perfectly suited to your favorite Merlot.

Ingredients

1/4 cup · 50 mL		olive oil
6		medium lamb shanks
1/2 cup · 125 mL		onion, chopped
1/2 cup · 125 mL		carrot, chopped
1/4 cup · 50 mL		celery, chopped
1		leek (white part only), chopped
1 clove		garlic, chopped
4		tomatoes, peeled, seeded and chopped
1		bay leaf
2 sprigs		thyme
2 sprigs		rosemary
2 cups · 500 mL		white wine
2 cups · 500 mL		Chicken Stock (page 267)
		kosher salt and white pepper to taste

Heat the olive oil in a large pot over medium-high heat. Add the shanks and cook, turning frequently, until all sides are golden brown, about 10 minutes.

Remove the shanks from the pan and add the onion, carrot, celery, leek and garlic. Reduce the heat to moderate and sauté the vegetables, stirring frequently, for about 5 minutes, or until golden brown.

Return the shanks to the pot along with all the cooking juices that have seeped out of the meat. Add the tomatoes, herbs, white wine and stock. Bring to a boil then reduce the heat to a simmer. Cook for 3–4 hours at a simmer until the meat separates from the bone and is fork tender. If at any point the meat begins to show through, add enough water to cover.

Remove the shanks from the pot and let cool to room temperature. Gently strip the lamb meat from the shank bones. Discard the bone and chop the meat into 1-inch (2-cm) pieces. Refrigerate the lamb until required.

MAKES 6 SERVINGS

recipe continued on next page

Ingredients

2 Tbsp.	•	30 mL	olive oil
2 cloves			garlic, minced
1			onion, chopped
4 cups	•	1 L	tomatoes, good-quality canned tomatoes
2 tsp.	•	10 mL	chipotle pepper in adobo (or substitute chili peppers to taste)
2 tsp.	•	10 mL	tomato paste
1 cup	•	250 mL	white wine
			kosher salt and white pepper to taste
1 Tbsp.	•	15 mL	basil, shredded
1 tsp.	•	5 mL	oregano, chopped
2 tsp.	•	10 mL	thyme, chopped

for the spicy tomato sauce

In a large saucepan, heat the olive oil over medium-high heat. Add the garlic and onion and sauté until the onion is light brown. Add the tomatoes, pepper and tomato paste; stir well. Add the wine and season with salt and pepper. Simmer the sauce for 1 hour, or until it has thickened. Add the herbs at the last moment and stir. Reserve until required.

to serve

3 cups	• 750 mL	**penne noodles, blanched**
2 cups	• 500 mL	**braised lamb shanks, chopped**
2 cups	• 500 mL	**spicy tomato sauce (page 226)**
6		**eggs, hard boiled, peeled and halved**
2 cups	• 500 mL	**spinach, stems removed**
1 cup	• 250 mL	**grated mozzarella cheese**
1 cup	• 250 mL	**grated Asiago cheese**
		kosher salt and white pepper to taste

Preheat oven to 375°F (190°C).

In a large bowl combine the blanched penne noodles with the braised lamb shanks, spicy tomato sauce, hard boiled eggs, spinach and cheeses. Season with salt and pepper and stir to combine.

Transfer to a casserole and bake for 40 minutes or until heated through. Serve.

Ingredients

1 cup	• 250 mL	**Chicken Stock (page 267)**
1 cup	• 250 mL	**whole milk**
3 Tbsp.	• 45 mL	**kosher salt**
1½ cups	• 375 mL	**cornmeal, medium ground**
2 Tbsp.	• 30 mL	**unsalted butter**
⅓ cup	• 75 mL	**olive oil**
½ cup	• 125 mL	**shaved Parmesan cheese**

Wild Mushroom Polenta
with Tomato Sauce

This recipe is meant to be enjoyed as a meatless entrée but I must say that it is also a delicious accompaniment to a venison roast or a grilled veal chop. When polenta bubbles it can cause a burn, so always use the lowest temperature possible and remember to stir, stir, stir!

In a medium saucepan combine the stock and milk. Season with salt and bring to a boil over high heat. Reduce the heat to a gentle simmer and add the cornmeal in a steady stream, stirring continuously with a wooden spoon. Continue stirring until the cornmeal becomes silky smooth, about 30 minutes, then stir in the butter, cover and keep warm.

to serve

Spoon the polenta into warm soup bowls. Top with the mushrooms and the tomato sauce (see next page). Drizzle with olive oil and shaved Parmesan and serve.

MAKES 6 SERVINGS

Ingredients

¼ cup	•	50 mL	**olive oil**
2 lbs.	•	1 kg	**wild mushrooms, chopped**
1			**shallot, finely diced**
1 clove			**garlic, finely diced**
½ cup	•	125 mL	**Merlot**
2 Tbsp.	•	30 mL	**chives, finely chopped**
1 Tbsp.	•	15 mL	**rosemary, finely chopped**
2 Tbsp.	•	30 mL	**balsamic vinegar**
1 Tbsp.	•	15 mL	**unsalted butter**
			kosher salt and white pepper to taste

for the mushrooms

Heat a large sauté pan over high heat and add the olive oil.
When the oil is hot, add the mushrooms and cook for 5 minutes,
stirring frequently. Add the shallot and garlic and stir. Add
the Merlot, bring to a boil, reduce the heat and simmer until
the wine has almost evaporated. Add the herbs, balsamic
vinegar, butter and salt and pepper. Set aside and keep warm.

Ingredients

6			**beefsteak tomatoes, peeled, seeded and chopped**
¼ cup	•	50 mL	**olive oil**
2 cloves			**garlic, finely chopped**
2			**shallots, finely minced**
2 tsp.	•	10 mL	**thyme, finely chopped**
1 tsp.	•	5 mL	**rosemary, finely chopped**
1 tsp.	•	5 mL	**sherry wine vinegar**
			kosher salt and white pepper to taste
3 leaves			**basil, finely shredded**

Tomato Sauce

In a large bowl, combine the tomatoes with the olive oil, garlic,
shallots, thyme and rosemary. Season with salt and pepper.
Combine then marinate at room temperature for 30 minutes.

Caribou Osso Buco

I enjoy preparing classical Italian recipes but I cannot reist turning them into something totally my own. Osso Bucco is a classical northern Italian recipe. I have made this mainstay of Italian cuisine into a dish more reflective of our Canadian wine country. By using caribou shank, sourced from Baffin Island, and a rich Merlot, one with a few years on it to expose the influence of oak aging, the Italian classic has become a Niagara classic.

Ingredients

6			caribou shanks, center cut, 1–2 inches (2.5-cm) thick
½ cup	•	125 mL	vegetable oil
2 cups	•	500 mL	all-purpose flour
1 Tbsp.	•	15 mL	kosher salt
2 tsp.	•	10 mL	ground black pepper
pinch			cayenne pepper
3 Tbsp.	•	45 mL	unsalted butter
½ cup	•	125 mL	onion, finely diced
2 tsp.	•	10 mL	garlic, finely diced
½ cup	•	125 mL	celery, finely diced
½ cup	•	125 mL	carrot, finely diced
½ cup	•	125 mL	leek (white part only), finely diced
½ cup	•	125 mL	fennel, finely diced
1 Tbsp.	•	15 mL	tomato paste
2 cups	•	500 mL	Merlot
4 cups	•	1 L	Chicken Stock (page 267)
2 tsp.	•	10 mL	rosemary, chopped
2 tsp.	•	10 mL	sage, chopped
2 tsp.	•	10 mL	thyme, chopped
2 Tbsp.	•	30 mL	parsley, chopped
2 Tbsp.	•	30 mL	unsalted butter

Preheat oven to 350°F (180°C).

Add the vegetable oil to a large sauté pan set over high heat. Whisk together the flour with the salt and pepper. Dredge each caribou shank in the seasoned flour and shake off any excess. Place each caribou shank in the hot oil and cook until golden brown, about 4 minutes per side. When all the shanks are browned remove them from the pan and keep warm.

In the same sauté pan over medium heat, melt 3 Tbsp. (45 mL) of butter.

When the butter is frothy, add the onion, garlic, celery, carrot, leek and fennel.

Cook for 15 minutes, stirring frequently, until the vegetables have browned slightly. Place the seared caribou shanks on the bed of vegetables and stir in the tomato paste, Merlot and chicken stock. Increase the heat to high and bring to a boil. Reduce the heat and simmer for $1\frac{1}{2}$ to 2 hours, or until the meat starts to fall off the bone.

Using a slotted spoon, gently lift the caribou shanks out of the simmering stock and keep warm. Pour the stock through a sieve into another pot and bring to simmer. Reduce the stock by half its volume. Add the herbs and 2 Tbsp. (30 mL) of butter and return the shanks to the sauce. Serve the caribou osso buco with Garlic Sauté Rapini on warmed plates.

MAKES 6 SERVINGS

Ingredients

$\frac{1}{4}$ cup	50 mL	**olive oil**
1 clove		**garlic**
3 cups	750 mL	**cleaned rapini, stems and leaves discarded**
$\frac{1}{4}$ cup	50 mL	**Chardonnay**
		kosher salt and white pepper to taste

Garlic Sauté Rapini

In a large sauté pan set over low heat, add the olive oil and the garlic. Cook until the garlic is slightly browned. Add the rapini and let it cook slowly. Add the white wine and cover the pan with a lid. When the liquid has evaporated, season with salt and pepper and remove from the heat. Serve immediately.

MAKES 6 SERVINGS

Ingredients

2 Tbsp. • 30 mL	**olive oil**
1	**onion, finely chopped**
1	**carrot, finely chopped**
1	**leek (white part only), finely chopped**
2 cloves	**garlic, crushed**
2	**bay leaves**
1 Tbsp. • 15 mL	**cracked black peppercorns**
2 tsp. • 10 mL	**ginger, chopped**
6	**pheasant legs, skin removed**
1 tsp. • 5 mL	**tomato paste**
2 cups • 500 mL	**Merlot**
2 cups • 500 mL	**Chicken Stock (page 267)**

Orecchiette
with Pheasant, Swiss Chard and Blue Cheese

This is a delicious combination of braised pheasant, Swiss chard and blue cheese in a rich pheasant broth. You may have noticed that I enjoy recipes that require long cooking times in low-temperature ovens. This is true personally and professionally. Braising foods is my favorite way to cook in the winter. It usually involves meats that are less expensive, lots of quality time in the kitchen with my kids and a delicious reward for our efforts.

Preheat oven to 300°F (150°C).

Add the olive oil to a large ovenproof sauté pan set over medium-high heat. Add the onion, carrot, leek, garlic, bay leaves, black peppercorns and ginger. Sauté for 15 minutes or until the vegetables have browned slightly. Place the pheasant legs on top of the vegetables and add the tomato paste, Merlot and stock. Bring the liquid to a boil, then carefully transfer the sauté pan to the oven. Bake the pheasant for 2–3 hours or until the meat falls off the bones. Remove the sauté pan from the oven and let cool at room temperature.

When the pheasant legs are cool enough to handle, pick the meat from the bones and discard the bones. Refrigerate the pheasant meat until required.

Strain the pheasant braising liquid through a fine mesh sieve into a small saucepan. Reserve this liquid until required. There should be 1–2 cups (250–500 mL) of liquid remaining.

MAKES 6 SERVINGS

Ingredients

2 Tbsp.	·	30 mL	**olive oil**
2 Tbsp.	·	30 mL	**unsalted butter**
6			**shallots, thinly sliced**
2 cups	·	500 mL	**reserved pheasant meat**
3 cups	·	750 mL	**Swiss chard (leaves only), chopped**
¼ cup	·	50 mL	**green onions, chopped**
1 Tbsp.	·	15 mL	**thyme, chopped**
2 cups	·	500 mL	**reserved braising liquid**
6 cups	·	1.5 L	**orecchiette noodles, blanched**
			kosher salt and white pepper to taste
¼ cup	·	50 mL	**blue cheese**

for the orecchiette noodles

Add the olive oil and butter to a large sauté pan set over medium-high heat. When the butter is frothy, add the shallots and cook until golden brown, about 2 minutes. Stir, then add the pheasant meat and the Swiss chard. Toss to combine the pheasant and chard, then add the green onions, thyme and braising liquid.

Bring the liquid to a boil then reduce the heat and simmer for 5 minutes, or until the sauce has reduced slightly. Add the orecchiette and toss with the pheasant and the chard. Season with salt and pepper. Stir in the blue cheese and serve in bowls before the cheese has a chance to melt completely.

Ingredients

³/₄ cup	• 175 mL	**icewine**
2 lbs.	• 1 kg	**elk tenderloin, divided into 6 portions**
1 Tbsp.	• 15 mL	**unsalted butter**
1 Tbsp.	• 15 mL	**olive oil**
		kosher salt and white pepper to taste

Icewine Elk Tenderloin
with Chanterelles and Red Currants

This dish was created for our annual icewine makers' dinner. J.L. Groux challenged me to create a menu featuring icewine in every course and this was my entrée. Icewine is one of the world's great ingredients, in the same category as other luxurious products like foie gras, truffles and caviar. The ingredients in this recipe are expensive, so follow the instructions exactly.

Place the icewine in a small pot over medium heat and bring to a boil. Reduce the heat to a simmer and reduce the wine until it becomes very syrupy and thick, about 15 minutes. Reserve the reduced icewine in a warm spot to keep it from thickening too much.

Heat the butter and olive oil in a large sauté pan over medium-high heat. When the butter is frothy, season the tenderloin with salt and pepper and add it to the sauté pan.

Cook for 8 minutes without turning and, using a pastry brush dipped into the icewine syrup, brush the elk frequently.

Using kitchen tongs, carefully turn the elk tenderloin over and cook for another 5 minutes, brushing the icewine glaze over the meat until it is all used.

Turn off the heat and keep the meat warm.

MAKES 6 SERVINGS

Ingredients

2 Tbsp.	•	30 mL	**unsalted butter**
1			**shallot, finely chopped**
½ cup	•	125 mL	**red currants**
½ cup	•	125 mL	**veal stock**
2 Tbsp.	•	30 mL	**icewine**
2 tsp.	•	10 mL	**champagne vinegar**
			kosher salt and white pepper to taste

for the red currant icewine sauce

In a small saucepan set over medium heat, heat 1 Tbsp. (15 mL) of the butter until frothy. Add the shallot and sauté until it has wilted, about 5 minutes. Add half the currants and the veal stock and simmer until syrupy, about 10 minutes. Pass the sauce through a fine mesh sieve into another small saucepan.

Return the sauce to a gentle simmer and add the remaining butter, red currants, champagne vinegar and salt and pepper. Keep warm until required.

Ingredients

1 Tbsp.	•	15 mL	**unsalted butter**
1 Tbsp.	•	15 mL	**olive oil**
1 cup	•	250 mL	**fingerling potatoes, blanched**
1 cup	•	250 mL	**chanterelle or hedgehog mushrooms**
⅓ cup	•	75 mL	**dried apricots, cut into slivers**
⅓ cup	•	75 mL	**sliced toasted almonds**
½ cup	•	125 mL	**icewine**
½ cup	•	125 mL	**stock (Mushroom Vegetable, page 43, or light Chicken, page 267)**
12 leaves			**basil, cut into chiffonade**
			kosher salt and white pepper to taste

for the mushroom sauté

Heat a sauté pan over moderately high heat and add the butter and oil. When the butter is frothy, add the fingerling potatoes and stir for a few minutes. Add the mushrooms and stir again before adding the apricots and almonds.

Stir in the icewine and reduce until it has almost all evaporated. Add the stock and basil and season with salt and pepper.

Serve the elk with red currant sauce and a generous spoonful of mushroom sauté.

Ingredients

12		**prosciutto slices**
12 leaves		**sage**
2 lbs. ·	1 kg	**beef tenderloin, divided into 6 portions**
pinch		**ground white pepper**
2 Tbsp. ·	30 mL	**olive oil**

Beef and Sage Medallions
with Sweet Potato Chips

Here is a way to jazz up a premium cut of meat. The prosciutto wrapping and the hazelnut crust produce a delicious balance between savory, salty, toasty and crunchy. Prosciutto wrapping is popular in my repertoire of recipes; I enjoy the delicate saltiness a slice of prosciutto can impart to veal, beef, game and even halibut, scallops and salmon.

Preheat oven to 400°F (200°C).

Lay the prosciutto on a cutting surface in 6 piles of 2 slices. Working with 1 group of prosciutto at a time, place 2 pieces of prosciutto side by side, slightly overlapping. Place 2 sage leaves on top of the prosciutto. Fold the prosciutto in half over the sage to make a long thin strip, no wider than the height of the beef. Place the beef on its side at one end of the prosciutto and roll to form a collar around the beef. Repeat with the remaining prosciutto and beef medallions.

Place an ovenproof sauté pan over moderate heat and add the olive oil. Sprinkle the beef with pepper and place the medallions in the sauté pan. Cook for 3 minutes, turn the beef medallions over and top with a heaping pile of hazelnut crust (page 237). Place the sauté pan in the oven and cook the beef for another 6 minutes or until done to your preference. Remove from the oven and serve with sweet potato chips (page 237).

MAKES 6 SERVINGS

Ingredients

¹⁄₂ cup	•	125 mL	**toasted chopped hazelnuts**
¹⁄₄ cup	•	50 mL	**bread crumbs**
2 Tbsp.	•	30 mL	**grated Parmesan cheese**
2 Tbsp.	•	30 mL	**Italian parsley, chopped**
1 Tbsp.	•	15 mL	**honey**
2 Tbsp.	•	30 mL	**Dijon mustard**
1 Tbsp.	•	15 mL	**olive oil**
			kosher salt and white pepper to taste

for the hazelnut crust

Combine all the ingredients thoroughly and reserve.

Ingredients

6 cups	•	1.5 L	**vegetable or peanut oil**
³⁄₄ cup	•	175 mL	**water**
¹⁄₄ cup	•	50 mL	**sparkling wine**
1 tsp.	•	5 mL	**baking powder**
2 cups	•	500 mL	**all-purpose flour**
1 tsp.	•	5 mL	**sesame oil**
			kosher salt and white pepper to taste
3			**sweet potatoes, peeled and cut into large french fries**

Sweet Potato Chips

Heat the oil in a deep fryer to 350°F (180°C).

In a large mixing bowl, combine the water, wine, baking powder, flour, sesame oil and seasonings. Cover the bowl with plastic wrap and set aside to rest for 10 minutes.

Working with one fry at a time, dip each sweet potato fry into the batter and transfer immediately into the hot oil. Cook until golden brown, 3–5 minutes.

Transfer the fried potato from the oil onto a kitchen towel to absorb excess oil. Serve with the beef medallions topped with hazelnut crust.

Spring

Beef Tenderloin
  with Walnut, Brie
  and Morel Salad

Halibut
  Poached in Red Wine

Barrel Maker's Stew

Summer

New York Striploin Steak
  with Cabernet Dried Cherry Butter

Linguine
  with Beef Striploin, Black Olives
  and Tomatoes

Venison Burger
  with Eggplant and Oka

Cabernet

CABERNET SAUVIGNON IS ONE OF THE WORLD'S MOST FAMOUS grape varietals. Its presence is most famously noticeable in the great Bordeaux wines of France—the wines you hear about that sell for thousands of dollars per bottle, or perhaps ones that are 60 or 70 years old. It is the grape which, when blended with Merlot, Cabernet Franc and/or Malbec, produces what is known as the Bordeaux blend, or meritage.

Cabernet Sauvignon wines are typically full-bodied wines containing tannin. Tannin is a substance found in the skins, stems and seeds of grapes. Tannin, while adding astringency when the wine is young, is an important ingredient enabling wine to age gracefully into greater complexity with full body, great depth of flavor and an elegant bouquet.

Cabernet Sauvignon is grown successfully in many countries, including Australia, Chile, Italy, Canada and the United States. The Cabernet Sauvignon wine made in California, some people claim, rivals the best of Bordeaux and is often more expensive. Cabernet Sauvignon is a small berry with a tough outer skin, which makes it less likely to be damaged by seasonal factors such as late autumn rains. It requires a temperate and dry climate with a relatively long growing season.

At Hillebrand Estates, Cabernet Sauvignon is blended with Merlot and Cabernet Franc to produce our most popular wine, Trius Red or Trius Grand Red. Every year, our wine maker tastes each of these wines independently and decides on the exact proportion of each to blend together into the Trius wines. Merlot contributes

Autumn

Prosciutto-Wrapped Caribou Tenderloin
with Morel Cream and Seedlings

Veal Tenderloin
with Foie Gras Mousse

Five-Spice and Peppercorn Crusted
Venison

Winter

Eggplant, Tomato and Red Pepper Bisque
with Aged Gouda

Cabernet Poached Bison Tenderloin
with Onion Marmalade

Cavatappi
with Veal Shank, Swiss Chard
and Dragon's Breath

Oven-Roasted Portobello Mushrooms
with Red Wine Blue Cheese Sauce

Sauvignon

softness and suppleness, Cabernet Franc adds complexity and Cabernet Sauvignon adds the structure and cellaring potential. I have been fortunate to taste a great deal of this meritage wine and continue to be amazed at the influence of each grape on the end result.

Cabernet Sauvignon has a flavor profile described as black currant, cassis and blackberry. It can exhibit herbaceous qualities such as bell peppers, asparagus and green olives, and spice such as ginger and peppercorns. Cabernet Sauvignon is always aged in oak and for this reason it can develop vanilla and coconut flavors, a smokiness and toastiness, and a taste of cedar, mushrooms, leather and tobacco.

In this chapter, Cabernet Sauvignon is represented through innovative food and wine pairings and also as an important ingredient in the cuisine. Cabernet Sauvignon can be enjoyed with many foods such as game, beef and aged cheese, all of which play major roles in wine country cuisine.

Ingredients

2 lbs.	•	1 kg	beef tenderloin, divided into 6 medallions
			kosher salt and white pepper to taste
1 Tbsp.	•	15 mL	olive oil
1 Tbsp.	•	15 mL	unsalted butter
¼ cup	•	50 mL	chopped walnuts
6 oz.	•	175 g	Brie, cut into 12 slices

Beef Tenderloin
with Walnut, Brie and Morel Salad

I love the baby lettuce that is available in the spring. One of my favorites is the arugula grown by Dave Perkins of Wyndam Farms. Initially this recipe was served as a salad without meat but one day I spontaneously added a bit of leftover roast beef and the result was a more festive and sophisticated salad.

Preheat oven to 450°F (230°C).

Season the beef with salt and pepper. Heat a sauté pan over medium-high heat and add the oil and butter. When the butter is frothy, add the beef tenderloin and sear on one side for 5 minutes. Remove the beef from the pan and place on an oven-proof baking sheet, raw-side down. Reserve the pan used to sear the meat.

Place the beef in the oven and cook for 5 minutes. Remove from the oven and top the medallions with equal portions of chopped walnuts. Top each piece of beef with the Brie slices in a criss-cross pattern on the walnuts. Return to the oven and continue cooking for 2 minutes longer, or until the Brie has melted slightly. Remove from the oven and keep warm.

MAKES 6 SERVINGS
recipe continued on next page

Ingredients

1 Tbsp.	•	15 mL	black peppercorns
3 sprigs			thyme
3 sprigs			rosemary
3 sprigs			parsley
2			bay leaves

Bouquet Garni

Place the spices on a small square of cheesecloth and tie the ends with kitchen string.

Ingredients

1 Tbsp. •	15 mL	**unsalted butter**
1 Tbsp. •	15 mL	**olive oil**
1/4 cup •	50 mL	**1/2-inch (1-cm) slices of smoked bacon**
1		**shallot, finely chopped**
2 cloves		**garlic, finely chopped**
2 cups •	500 mL	**morel mushrooms, chopped**
1 cup •	250 mL	**Cabernet Sauvignon**
1/2 cup •	125 mL	**veal jus (page 243)**
2 Tbsp. •	30 mL	**unsalted butter**
1 Tbsp. •	15 mL	**rosemary, chopped**

for the morels

Return the pan used to sear the beef to medium-high heat. Add the 1 Tbsp. (15 mL) of butter and the olive oil and when the butter is frothy, add the bacon. Stir for a few minutes, then add the shallot, garlic and mushrooms. When the mushrooms have wilted, after about 2 minutes, add the red wine. Reduce until only 1/2 cup (125 mL) of wine remains.

Add the veal jus and reduce until only 1/4 cup (50 mL) of liquid remains. Add the 2 Tbsp. (30 mL) of butter and the rosemary, stirring to melt the butter into the sauce.

Serve the beef tenderloin topped with morels, on a bed of rocket salad.

Ingredients

3 Tbsp. •	45 mL	**olive oil**
1 tsp. •	5 mL	**almond oil**
1 Tbsp. •	15 mL	**sherry wine vinegar**
1		**shallot, finely chopped**
		kosher salt and white pepper to taste
pinch		**granulated sugar**
1/4 cup •	50 mL	**sliced almonds, toasted**
3 cups •	750 mL	**rocket (arugula)**

for the salad

Combine the olive and almond oils in a small bowl. Add the sherry wine vinegar and shallot and season to taste with salt, pepper and a pinch of sugar.

Combine the almonds with the rocket and toss together. Drizzle the dressing over top.

Ingredients

10 lbs.	•	4.5 kg	**veal bones**
3			**onions, chopped**
4			**celery stalks, chopped**
2			**leeks, chopped**
4			**carrots, peeled and chopped**
1 lb.	•	500 g	**white mushrooms**
3 Tbsp.	•	45 mL	**tomato paste**
1			**bouquet garni (page 241)**
3 cups	•	750 mL	**red wine**

Veal Jus

Veal jus is the end result of long-simmered veal bones, vegetables and water. It is the foundation upon which most of our kitchen's meat sauces are based. A good veal jus will be rich, smooth and free of impurities. It should have a subtle meaty flavor with no bitterness. Good jus is a great conductor of other flavors such as wine, mushrooms, tomato and mustard.

Rinse the veal bones in several changes of cold water. Transfer the bones to a large pot and cover with cold water. The water should cover the veal bones by at least 4 inches (10 cm). Turn the heat to low and let the water come slowly to a simmer. Carefully skim off any impurities that rise to the surface.

When the bones have come to a gentle simmer, and the impurities have been skimmed away, combine the onion, celery, leek, carrot and mushrooms in a colander and wash them under cold water. Pour the vegetables into the simmering pot and let the stock return to a gentle simmer. Add the tomato paste and the bouquet garni. Do not let the stock boil too rapidly as this will cause it to become cloudy and unpleasant.

Continue simmering the veal bones for 8 hours. The stock will gradually turn golden brown. Keep skimming the surface to remove the impurities every hour or so. Do not let the stock boil too rapidly which would bring out the bitterness and reduce your yield.

Remove the veal stock from the heat and let it stand for 30 minutes. Using a ladle, carefully transfer the veal stock through a strainer into another pot. Discard the bones.

Pour the red wine into a large stockpot and reduce the wine over medium heat, until thick and syrupy. Add the veal stock and simmer over medium heat until thick and syrupy. Refrigerate the veal jus in a clean container until required. For 10 lbs. (4.5 kg) of veal bones, the yield on this recipe will be 12–20 cups (3–5 L) of finished sauce. It freezes well in zip lock bags for up to 6 months.

Halibut Poached in Red Wine

This technique of poaching white fish in red wine may seem unconventional and it will probably raise a few eyebrows. The dramatic presentation and lovely flavor are unforgettable. The key to this recipe is to use super-fresh halibut; any sign of fishiness from taste to smell will upset the balance of this recipe.

Ingredients

1 Tbsp.	·	15 mL	**unsalted butter**
1 Tbsp.	·	15 mL	**olive oil**
1			**bay leaf**
2 tsp.	·	10 mL	**mustard seeds**
2 tsp.	·	10 mL	**white peppercorns**
2			**shallots, finely diced**
¹⁄₂ cup	·	125 mL	**carrot, finely chopped**
¹⁄₂ cup	·	125 mL	**celery, finely chopped**
¹⁄₂ cup	·	125 mL	**shiitake mushrooms, finely chopped**
2			**tomatoes, seeded and finely chopped**
2 Tbsp.	·	30 mL	**honey**
3 cups	·	750 mL	**Cabernet Sauvignon**
1 cup	·	250 mL	**Fish Stock (page 50)**
2 Tbsp.	·	30 mL	**verjus (or red wine vinegar)**
			kosher salt and white pepper to taste
2 lbs.	·	1 kg	**halibut fillets, divided into 6 portions**
1 Tbsp.	·	15 mL	**unsalted butter**
2			**lemons, zest of, blanched**
1 Tbsp.	·	15 mL	**Italian parsley, finely chopped**
1 Tbsp.	·	15 mL	**capers, rinsed and finely chopped**
1 tsp.	·	5 mL	**fleur de sel**

Heat a saucepan over medium heat and add the 1 Tbsp. (15 mL) butter and the oil. When the butter has completely melted add the bay leaf, mustard seeds and white peppercorns. Add the shallots, carrot, celery, shiitake mushroom and tomatoes.

Cook, stirring frequently, for about 5 minutes, or until the vegetables begin to wilt slightly. Stir in the honey to coat the vegetables. Add the wine, stock and verjus. Bring to a boil and reduce the liquid to about 1 cup (250 mL).

Reduce the heat to a simmer. Season the halibut with salt and pepper and add to the stock. Poach for 7 minutes, or until the fish is opaque. Using a slotted spoon, remove the halibut from the poaching liquid and reserve.

Strain the liquid through a sieve into a bowl and discard the vegetables. Increase the heat, return the liquid to the saucepan and bring it to a boil. Reduce the liquid until just $\frac{1}{2}$ cup (125 mL) remains. Add 1 Tbsp. (15 mL) of butter and stir until it melts.

Return the halibut to the pan and spoon the reduced liquid over top. Cook for 2–3 minutes, or until the halibut is warmed through. Combine the lemon zest, parsley, capers and fleur de sel in a small pile on top of the halibut.

Place the fish on warm serving plates and drizzle with the red wine glaze to serve.

MAKES 6 SERVINGS

1 lb.	500 g	**beef top sirloin, cut into 1-inch (2.5-cm) cubes**
		kosher salt and white pepper to taste
2 Tbsp.	30 mL	**paprika**
1 tsp.	5 mL	**ground ginger**
1/4 cup	50 mL	**vegetable oil**
2 Tbsp.	30 mL	**unsalted butter**
1 cup	250 mL	**pearl onions, peeled and blanched**
1/4 cup	50 mL	**smoked bacon, chopped**
1 Tbsp.	15 mL	**garlic, chopped**
2 cups	500 mL	**Cabernet Sauvignon**
1/2 cup	125 mL	**veal jus (page 243)**
1 Tbsp.	15 mL	**unsalted butter**
1 tsp.	5 mL	**rosemary, chopped**
1 tsp.	5 mL	**sage, chopped**
1 tsp.	5 mL	**Italian parsley, chopped**

Barrel Maker's Stew

This recipe was created in honor of the coopers who craft the oak barrels used to age wine. It is a classically inspired recipe that uses a full bodied and tannic Cabernet Sauvignon as its base flavor. The barrel maker's stew has become, by far, the best-selling lunch item on our menus. It is a quick recipe to prepare if the mis en place is ready in advance.

In a large bowl season the beef with salt and pepper, then add the paprika and ginger.

Heat a large sauté pan over medium-high heat and add the vegetable oil.

Brown the beef well on all sides, about 20 minutes. Using a slotted spatula, remove the meat and set aside.

Discard the oil in the pan and add the 2 Tbsp. (30 mL) of butter. When the butter is frothy, add the pearl onions. Cook for about 10 minutes, stirring frequently until the onions have browned slightly. Add the bacon and sauté with the onions until the bacon has crisped slightly. Remove the onions and bacon and reserve.

Drain off any excess butter and bacon fat and add the garlic, stirring until it browns, about 5 minutes. Add the Cabernet Sauvignon and bring to a boil.

Reduce the heat to medium and simmer until the wine has reduced to 1/2 cup (125 mL). Add the veal jus and return to a boil.

Reduce the heat to a simmer and return the meat, bacon and onions to the pan. Add the 1 Tbsp. (15 mL) butter and the chopped herbs, stirring to melt the butter into the sauce. Serve.

Ingredients

¼ cup	•	50 mL	**vegetable oil**
5 lbs.	•	2.2 kg	**New York striploin, divided into 6 equal portions**
			kosher salt and white pepper to taste

New York Striploin Steak
with Cabernet Dried Cherry Butter

This steak needs to be cut thick because when you eat a New York striploin only a thick steak (cooked medium-rare, in my opinion) will do. The Cabernet dried cherry butter is a worthwhile staple that can be kept in the freezer and sliced as you need it. Try making it with other dried fruits such as dried apricots, cranberries or pears.

Preheat oven to 500°F (260°C).

This recipe will taste even better if you have a well-seasoned cast iron pan, but at least use a large, heavy-bottomed sauté pan. In either case, set the pan over medium-high heat. Add the vegetable oil.

Rub the steaks with the salt and pepper and carefully place the meat in the pan. Sear, without turning the meat, for 7 minutes. Turn the meat over and sear for another 2 minutes.

Transfer the pan to the oven and cook for 5 minutes, or to your preferred degree of doneness.

MAKES 6 SERVINGS

Ingredients

1 cup	·	250 mL	**Cabernet Sauvignon**
1 Tbsp.	·	15 mL	**red wine vinegar**
2 cups	·	500 mL	**dried cherries**
1 lb.	·	500 g	**unsalted butter**
2 Tbsp.	·	30 mL	**rosemary, finely chopped**
1 Tbsp.	·	15 mL	**kosher salt**

Cabernet Dried Cherry Butter

Pour the wine into a small saucepan set over medium heat and bring to a boil. Simmer until the wine has reduced to a syrupy consistency, leaving only about 2 Tbsp. (30 mL) remaining, about 20 minutes. Let the reduced wine cool to room temperature.

Combine the remaining ingredients in a food mixer and mix thoroughly.

Add the reduced Cabernet Sauvignon and mix thoroughly until the butter is a pleasant pink color. Using a rubber spatula, scrape out the butter onto a large piece of parchment paper or plastic wrap. Roll the butter into a long tube and place it in the freezer to set.

When the butter is firm to the touch, but not frozen solid, remove it from the freezer, unroll it from the paper or plastic wrap and slice into 1-inch (2.5-cm) slices. Any extra butter may be kept, frozen and tightly wrapped, for up to 3 months.

Top each serving of steak with 1 or 2 slices of the cherry butter and a fresh sprinkling of kosher salt and black pepper.

Ingredients

3 lbs. ·	1.5 kg	**beef striploin steaks, divided into 6 equal portions**
2 Tbsp. ·	30 mL	**olive oil**
		kosher salt and white pepper to taste

Linguine with Beef Striploin,
Black Olives and Tomatoes

This recipe was created at home by accident one summer afternoon. My wife, Kaleen, was indoors preparing a fettuccine noodle dish with olives and tomatoes, while I was outside grilling some beautiful beef striploin steaks. When lunch was ready, I got to the kitchen and seized the opportunity to create this dish.

Heat a grill to medium-high.

Rub the beef with the olive oil and season with salt and pepper. Grill to the desired degree of doneness, 5–8 minutes per side.

MAKES 6 SERVINGS

recipe continued on next page

Ingredients

1 lb.	• 500 g	**linguine noodles, dry**
2 Tbsp.	• 30 mL	**olive oil**
1		**red onion, julienned**
2 cloves		**garlic, minced**
1 cup	• 250 mL	**cherry tomatoes, roughly chopped**
$\frac{1}{2}$ cup	• 125 mL	**black olives, roughly chopped**
$\frac{1}{4}$ cup	• 50 mL	**extra virgin olive oil**
1 Tbsp.	• 15 mL	**sliced sage leaves**

for the pasta sauce

Bring a large pot of salted water to a rapid boil. Add the linguine noodles and cook until *al dente,* about 10 minutes.

Using a large sauté pan set over moderate heat, add the 2 Tbsp. (30 mL) of olive oil. Sauté the onions in the oil for 5 minutes, or until they have substantially reduced in volume and have colored slightly. Add the tomatoes and stir to combine well with the onions. Add the black olives. Reduce the heat and add $\frac{1}{4}$ cup (50 mL) of olive oil and sage. Toss to combine and divide the noodles among 6 large dinner plates.

Slice each steak into thin strips and serve on the noodles.

Ingredients

2.25 lbs. •	1.2 kg	**venison shoulder or leg, ground**
½ lb. •	250 g	**pork, ground**
2		**eggs**
2 Tbsp. •	30 mL	**olive oil**
2 Tbsp. •	30 mL	**grainy mustard**
2 Tbsp. •	30 mL	**rosemary, chopped**
		kosher salt and white pepper to taste
1 tsp. •	5 mL	**cumin seed, ground**
1 tsp. •	5 mL	**ground ginger**
1 tsp. •	5 mL	**ground paprika**
1 tsp. •	5 mL	**ground coriander**

Venison Burger
with Eggplant and Oka

Oka cheese was first made by Canadian monks from the Prairies. It is a delicious semi-soft cheese with nuances of floral and nut. You won't find these burgers on any fast food menu, but your guests will appreciate the great flavor from the Oka and eggplant combination. The venison burger is lightly seasoned with Asian spices, which adds to the overall effect. Serve on over-sized onion buns.

Mix all the ingredients until well combined. Form the mix into 6 burgers and refrigerate until ready to grill.

to serve

Preheat grill to medium-high.

Place the venison burgers on the grill and cook to your desired degree of doneness, 8–10 minutes per side. When the venison patties are just about ready, place one eggplant and Oka cheese disk on each burger. Allow the cheese to melt slightly and serve.

MAKES 6 SERVINGS

recipe continued on next page

Ingredients

1		**eggplant, cut into 6 disks**
2 Tbsp. ·	30 mL	**kosher salt**
1 Tbsp. ·	15 mL	**olive oil**
1 clove		**garlic, finely chopped**
		kosher salt and white pepper to taste
6 slices		**Oka cheese**

for the eggplant

Sprinkle the eggplant with salt and allow to sit at room temperature for an hour. Rinse the salt from the eggplant under cold running water and pat dry. Brush the eggplant with olive oil on both sides. Sprinkle with garlic and season with salt and pepper.

Preheat oven to 475°F (240°C).

Place the eggplant on a baking tray and cook in the oven for 10 minutes per side. Remove and let cool slightly. Top each slice of eggplant with a slice of Oka.

Chef's Note

Serve with a side of mashed potatoes.

Ingredients

2 lbs.	·	1 kg	**caribou tenderloin, divided into 6 portions**
2 Tbsp.	·	30 mL	**grapeseed oil**
			kosher salt and white pepper to taste
6 leaves			**sage**
3			**red peppers, skinned and seeds removed**
6 slices			**prosciutto**

Prosciutto-Wrapped Caribou Tenderloin
with Morel Cream and Seedlings

This is the recipe you will want to make if you feel up to a culinary challenge. There are three elements to this dish: the meat, the sauce and the salad. I like serving composed and refined salads using seedlings and sprouts. Sometimes I don't serve any other vegetables with meat, relying only on the greens to provide the necessary contrast and flavor components.

Rub the venison with the grapeseed oil and season with salt and pepper.

Wrap the loins first with the sage, then with the red peppers and finally with the prosciutto. Secure with toothpicks or butcher's twine.

Refrigerate until ready to use.

to serve

Preheat oven to 375°F (190°C).

Cook the venison in the hot oven for 10 minutes, turning once after 5 minutes. Remove from the oven and let the meat rest for 5 minutes.

Slice the venison into neat medallions. Divide the salad (see next page) among 6 dinner plates. Spoon the mushroom sauce (next page) beside the salad, being careful not to pour it on the greens. Place the venison medallions on the mushroom sauce and serve.

MAKES 6 SERVINGS

recipe continued on next page

Ingredients

2 Tbsp.	• 30 mL	**olive oil**
2		**shallots, finely minced**
3 cups	• 750 mL	**morel mushrooms**
1 clove		**garlic, finely minced**
$\frac{1}{2}$ cup	• 125 mL	**Vegetable Mushroom Stock (page 43)**
$\frac{1}{2}$ cup	• 125 mL	**white wine**
$\frac{1}{2}$ cup	• 125 mL	**veal jus (page 243)**
$\frac{1}{2}$ cup	• 125 mL	**35% cream**
1 Tbsp.	• 15 mL	**truffle oil**
		kosher salt and white pepper to taste

for the sauce

In a small, heavy-bottomed saucepan, heat the olive oil over moderate heat. Add the shallots and sauté for 3 minutes without coloring. Add the mushrooms and cook until their liquid has evaporated, about 10 minutes. Add the garlic and mushroom stock and simmer until almost all of the stock has evaporated. Add the veal jus and cream and bring to a boil.

Using a hand-held blender, purée the mushrooms and cream. Add the truffle oil and process for 30 seconds. Season with salt and pepper and keep warm.

2		**lemons, juice of**
$\frac{1}{4}$ cup	• 50 mL	**sherry wine vinegar**
$\frac{1}{2}$ cup	• 125 mL	**olive oil**
		kosher salt and white pepper to taste
1 tsp.	• 5 mL	**oregano, finely chopped**
$\frac{1}{2}$ tsp.	• 2 mL	**cayenne pepper**
3 cups	• 750 mL	**sunflower seedlings**

for the salad

Combine all the ingredients, except the seedlings, and blend thoroughly to create an emulsion. Toss with the seedlings until well combined.

Ingredients

4 oz.	• 125 g	**chicken breast, skin removed, roughly chopped**
2 oz.	• 50 g	**foie gras**
1 oz.	• 25 g	**mushroom paste (page 263)**
³⁄₄ cup	• 175 mL	**35% cream**
		kosher salt and white pepper to taste
1 Tbsp.	• 15 mL	**rosemary, chopped**

Veal Tenderloin
with Foie Gras Mousse

The foie gras mousse used here as a topping for the veal can be modified with the addition of toasted seeds and nuts to be a stuffing for poultry. It will even taste great stuffed in tomatoes or on mushroom caps, or on its own formed into little barrel shapes and poached in a strong mushroom or chicken broth.

Place the chicken and foie gras in the bowl of a food processor and process to a semi-smooth paste. What you're looking for is a mixture that still has some texture.

Add the mushroom paste, cream and salt and pepper. Purée until smooth. Add the rosemary and mix well. Using a rubber spatula, remove the mousse from the bowl of the food processor and refrigerate until required.

MAKES 6 SERVINGS
recipe continued on next page

Ingredients

2 lbs.	•	1 kg	**veal tenderloins, divided into 6 equal portions, all visible fat removed**
			kosher salt and white pepper to taste
2 Tbsp.	•	30 mL	**olive oil (+ extra for seasoning)**
2 Tbsp.	•	30 mL	**unsalted butter**
3 oz.	•	90 g	**foie gras mousse (page 261)**

for the veal

Preheat oven to 375°F (190°C).

Season the veal with salt and pepper and olive oil. Top each piece of veal with some of the mousse.

In a large sauté pan over medium-high heat, warm the olive oil and butter.

When the butter is frothy, add the veal and sear until golden brown, about 5 minutes. Place the veal on a baking tray. Reserve the pan for the sauce.

Transfer the meat to the oven for 5 minutes or until desired degree of doneness. Keep warm.

Ingredients

1 cup	•	250 mL	**unsalted butter at room temperature**
3			**scallions, minced**
1 Tbsp.	•	15 mL	**horseradish**
1 tsp.	•	5 mL	**garlic, chopped**
2 Tbsp.	•	30 mL	**parsley, chopped**
dash			**soy sauce**
1			**lemon, juice of**
			kosher salt and white pepper to taste

for the scallion horseradish butter

Combine all the ingredients and scrape into a piping bag, or roll in plastic wrap into a log. Pipe out into rosettes, if you wish, and refrigerate until needed.

Ingredients

1 Tbsp.	•	15 mL	**unsalted butter**
2			**shallots, finely chopped**
½ cup	•	125 mL	**white wine**
½ cup	•	125 mL	**35% cream**
			kosher salt and white pepper to taste
1 Tbsp.	•	15 mL	**Dijon mustard**
2 Tbsp.	•	30 mL	**tarragon, chopped**
1			**lemon, juice of**

for the sauce

Return the pan used for searing the veal to the heat and add the butter.

When the butter is frothy, add the shallots and stir for 1 minute over moderately high heat. Add the white wine and let the liquid boil until reduced to 2 Tbsp. (30 mL). Add the cream and reduce until it coats the back of a spoon.

Season with salt and pepper and whisk in the mustard, tarragon and lemon juice. Whisk in the scallion horseradish butter and serve over the veal tenderloin.

Ingredients

2 Tbsp.	•	30 mL	**olive oil**
3 cups	•	750 mL	**mushrooms, cleaned and finely chopped**
1			**shallot, finely chopped**
1 clove			**garlic, finely chopped**
1 cup	•	250 mL	**red wine**
1 cup	•	250 mL	**Chicken Stock (page 267)**
½ cup	•	125 mL	**unsalted butter**
1 tsp.	•	5 mL	**truffle oil**
			kosher salt and white pepper to taste

for the mushroom paste

Heat the olive oil in a large sauté pan over medium-high heat and add the mushrooms, shallot and garlic. Stir frequently to prevent burning and to combine the flavors.

Add the red wine and stock and simmer until all the liquid has evaporated. Transfer the mushrooms to a food processor and purée until smooth. With the motor running add the butter and the truffle oil and season to taste. Transfer to a bowl and refrigerate until required.

Ingredients

2 Tbsp.	•	30 mL	**lemon zest, blanched and finely diced**
2 Tbsp.	•	30 mL	**lime zest, blanched and finely diced**
2 Tbsp.	•	30 mL	**black peppercorns, crushed**
2 Tbsp.	•	30 mL	**olive oil**
2 Tbsp.	•	30 mL	**unsalted butter**
2 lbs.	•	1 kg	**venison striploin, divided into 6 portions**
2 Tbsp.	•	30 mL	**maple syrup**
1 Tbsp.	•	15 mL	**ground five-spice powder**
			kosher salt to taste

Five-Spice
and Peppercorn Crusted Venison

I love the pungency of Chinese five-spice powder. In this recipe I add peppercorns and citrus peel to a five-spice mix and, with good old-fashioned Canadian maple syrup, create a glaze for delicious tender venison striploin steaks. It is the perfect meal for autumn entertaining.

Preheat oven to 400°F (200°C).

Combine the zest with the peppercorns.

In a sauté pan, heat the olive oil and butter until the butter is frothy. Sear the venison on all sides. Remove from the sauté pan and transfer to an ovenproof baking tray. Brush maple syrup all over the venison and sprinkle with the five-spice powder, salt and the peppercorn mixture.

Roast until medium-rare, about 10 minutes. Remove from the oven and let the meat rest for 5 minutes.

Slice the meat and top with balsamic glazed onions (page 265).

MAKES 6 SERVINGS

Ingredients

1 Tbsp. ·	15 mL	**olive oil**
1 Tbsp. ·	15 mL	**unsalted butter**
$\frac{1}{2}$ cup ·	125 mL	**pearl onions, peeled**
$\frac{1}{4}$ cup ·	50 mL	**balsamic vinegar**
		kosher salt and white pepper to taste
1 tsp. ·	5 mL	**lemon thyme, finely chopped**

for the balsamic glazed onions

In a large sauté pan set over medium heat add the olive oil and butter. When the butter is frothy add the onions and cook, stirring frequently, until they are a shiny brown, about 15 minutes.

Add the balsamic vinegar, salt and pepper and lemon thyme. Bring the vinegar to a boil then simmer until it is reduced by half and the onions are nicely glazed. Remove from the heat and let cool to room temperature.

HOW TO MAKE FIVE-SPICE POWDER

Make your own five-spice powder by combining equal parts of cinnamon, cloves, fennel seed, star anise and Chinese peppercorns in a spice mill.

Ingredients

3		**eggplants, each about 1 lb. (500 g)**
2 Tbsp.	30 mL	**kosher salt**
¼ cup	50 mL	**olive oil**
2 Tbsp.	30 mL	**unsalted butter**
1		**onion, diced**
¼ cup	50 mL	**roasted garlic purée (page 182)**
2 cup	500 mL	**red peppers, roasted and peeled**
1 cup	250 mL	**Tomato Sauce (page 229)**
1 cup	250 mL	**white wine**
4 cups	1L	**Chicken Stock (page 267)**
		kosher salt and white pepper to taste

Eggplant, Tomato and Red Pepper
Bisque with Aged Gouda

You may decide to make this full-flavored soup a lunch entrée because it is thick and rich. Few things are more satisfying with some crusty bread and a matching big-bodied Cabernet Sauvignon.

Cut each eggplant in half, lengthwise. Score the pulp in a cross-hatch pattern with a sharp knife. Sprinkle the salt over the eggplant pulp and allow to rest for 1 hour.

Preheat oven to 350°F (180°C).

Rinse the eggplant halves and gently squeeze the eggplant to drain any additional liquid. Rub the eggplant halves with the olive oil and place in a shallow baking pan. Bake for 25 minutes or until the eggplant is brown and tender.

In a large sauté pan set over medium heat melt the butter. When the butter is frothy, add the onion and cook, stirring, for 3 minutes. Add the eggplant, the roasted garlic purée, roasted red peppers and tomato sauce.

Stir in the white wine and chicken stock. Cover and simmer over low heat for 30 minutes.

Put the contents of the soup through a sieve. Purée the soup in a food processor until smooth. Return the soup to the pot and add the liquid until the soup is the desired consistency. Bring the soup to a simmer and adjust seasonings.

MAKES 6 SERVINGS

Ingredients

1			**day-old baguette**
1/4 cup	•	50 mL	**garlic oil (page 182)**
1/2 cup	•	125 mL	**grated Gouda**

for the Gouda garnish

Preheat oven to 350°F (180°C).

Cut the baguette into twelve 1-inch (2.5-cm) slices. Brush the baguette slices with the garlic oil and place in the oven for 5 minutes. Turn each piece over and toast for another 5 minutes.

Remove from the oven and top with equal portions of the grated Gouda. Return the croutons to the oven until the cheese has melted then serve on top of each bowl of soup.

Ingredients

10 lbs.	•	4.5 kg	**chicken bones**
16 cups	•	4 L	**water**
2			**onions, chopped**
1			**leeks (white part only), washed and chopped**
2			**carrots, peeled and chopped**
2 stalks			**celery, chopped**
2 cloves			**garlic, chopped**
2 lbs.	•	1 kg	**mushrooms**
2 cups	•	500 mL	**white wine**
1			**bouquet garni (page 241)**

Chicken Stock

In a large stockpot set over medium heat combine the bones and the water. Bring to a gentle boil, reduce the heat to a simmer and skim off any impurities that rise to the surface.

Add the remaining ingredients and simmer over low heat for 3 hours. Strain the stock through a fine mesh sieve and reserve refrigerated until required.

For a more pronounced stock flavor, roast the bones before beginning the recipe. To roast chicken bones, place them on an ovenproof tray in an oven preheated to 350°F (180°C) for 1 hour or until the bones are golden brown. Remove from the oven and discard the grease. Use the bones as directed above.

MAKES 16 CUPS/4 L

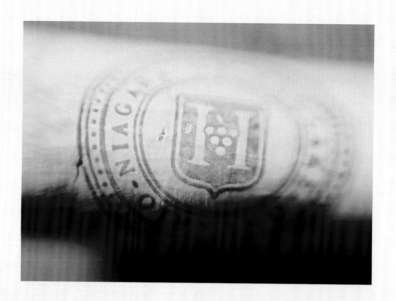

Cabernet Poached Bison Tenderloin
with Onion Marmalade

Bison meat is a staple in the Hillebrand restaurant. I like using this delicious meat because it cooks beautifully. Make sure you are using a good quality Cabernet Sauvignon for this recipe; the general rule of thumb when cooking with wine is to use only wine that is good enough to drink. The flaws in wines are magnified during the cooking process.

Ingredients

2 lbs.	• 1 kg	**bison tenderloin, cut into 6 portions**
		kosher salt and white pepper to taste

Season the bison with salt and pepper and reserve in the refrigerator.

MAKES 6 SERVINGS

recipe continued on next page

THE ART OF POACHING

Poaching meat is a very old culinary technique. The secret to maintaining a moist end result is to make sure the meat does not ever boil rapidly. The correct cooking rate is a gentle simmer, where the liquid is only slightly bubbling at the surface.

Ingredients

1 bottle		**Cabernet Sauvignon**
3		**shallots, chopped**
1		**carrot, peeled and chopped**
1		**leek (white part only), washed and chopped**
½ cup	· 125 mL	**mushrooms, chopped**
1		**bay leaf**
2 sprigs		**thyme**
2 sprigs		**rosemary**
2 cloves		**garlic, chopped**
2 Tbsp.	· 30 mL	**honey**
1 Tbsp.	· 15 mL	**kosher salt**

for the poaching liquid

Combine the ingredients in a large pot and bring to a boil over high heat.

Reduce the heat to a simmer for 10 minutes. Using a slotted spoon or strainer, remove the vegetables from the wine and discard. Return the wine to a gentle simmer.

Carefully immerse the bison into the simmering wine and let it cook for 8 minutes, or to your preferred degree of doneness. Using a slotted spoon, remove the tenderloin from the wine and serve.

Garnish with a sprinkle of kosher salt and the onion marmalade (page 271).

Ingredients

2 Tbsp.	•	30 mL	**olive oil**
2 Tbsp.	•	30 mL	**unsalted butter**
3			**onions, finely chopped**
$\frac{1}{4}$ tsp.	•	1 mL	**ground cumin**
$\frac{1}{4}$ tsp.	•	1 mL	**ground ginger**
$\frac{1}{4}$ tsp.	•	1 mL	**cayenne pepper**
1 tsp.	•	5 mL	**crushed black peppercorns**
$\frac{1}{4}$ tsp.	•	1 mL	**mustard seeds**
1 cup	•	250 mL	**Cabernet Sauvignon**
2 Tbsp.	•	30 mL	**honey**
			kosher salt and white pepper to taste

Onion Marmalade

Heat a large sauté pan over medium heat and add the olive oil and butter.

When the butter is frothy, add the onions. Stir frequently for 10 minutes or until the onions have become golden brown. Add the spices.

Continue to sauté for 5 more minutes, stirring frequently, then add the red wine and honey. Bring the wine to a boil and let it simmer, stirring frequently, until it has reduced to a syrupy consistency. Remove from the heat and let cool to room temperature. Season with salt and pepper.

MAKES 1 CUP/250 ML

Cavatappi with Veal Shank,
Swiss Chard and Dragon's Breath

Veal shank is a worthwhile choice for its unique flavor and low cost. Of course, my recipe includes a generous splash of Cabernet Sauvignon to help it along! Dragon's Breath is a unique blue veined cheese I discovered in Nova Scotia a couple of years ago while on holiday. It has become a signature on our cheese board.

Ingredients

1 cup	• 250 mL	all-purpose flour
1 Tbsp.	• 15 mL	kosher salt
1 Tbsp.	• 15 mL	black peppercorns, crushed
$^1/_4$ cup	• 50 mL	olive oil
3		veal shanks, each about 2 inches (5 cm) thick
2 Tbsp.	• 30 mL	butter
1		onion, chopped
2 cloves		garlic, chopped
1		carrot, peeled and chopped
1		leek (white part only), chopped
$^1/_4$ bulb		fennel (white part only), chopped
2 cups	• 500 mL	Cabernet Sauvignon
1 cup	• 250 mL	Chicken Stock (page 267)

Preheat oven to 300°F (150°C).

Combine the flour with the salt and pepper.

Add the olive oil to a large ovenproof sauté pan set over medium-high heat. Dredge the veal shanks in the seasoned flour and shake off any excess. Add the veal shank to the hot oil and brown on all sides. Remove the shanks from the oil and reserve.

Discard any oil left in the pan and set the pan back on medium-high heat.

Add the butter and when it's frothy add the onion and garlic. When slightly browned, or after about 5 minutes, add the carrot, leek and fennel. Stir frequently for another 5 minutes until all the vegetables have browned slightly.

Return the veal shanks to the pan. Cover the veal shanks and vegetables with the wine and stock. Bring the liquid to a boil, reduce the heat and simmer. Transfer the sauté pan to the oven and cook for 2–3 hours or until the meat is fork tender. Remove the pan from the oven and let cool to room temperature. Using a slotted spoon, lift the meat from the liquid and reserve.

Strain the liquid through a fine mesh sieve and return to medium-high heat in a small pot. Bring the liquid to a boil and reduce by half. Reserve the reduced liquid.

When the shanks are cool enough to handle, remove the meat from the bones. Discard the bones and reserve the meat.

MAKES 6 SERVINGS
recipe continued on next page

Ingredients

3 Tbsp. • 45 mL		**olive oil**
1 cup • 250 mL		**shiitake mushrooms, julienned**
1 tsp. • 5 mL		**garlic, minced**
2 cups • 500 mL		**Swiss chard, julienned**
2 cups • 500 mL		**veal shank meat**
1 cup • 250 mL		**veal shank reduced cooking liquid**
¼ cup • 50 mL		**tomatoes, chopped**
1 lb. • 500 g		**cavatappi noodles, blanched**
6 leaves		**basil, julienned**
1 Tbsp. • 15 mL		**unsalted butter**
4		**green onions, cut into 1-inch (2.5-cm) pieces**
½ lb. • 250 g		**Dragon's Breath, or other blue cheese**

for the cavatappi

In a large sauté pan, heat the olive oil and add the mushrooms. Cook the mushrooms for 5 minutes, stirring frequently, until well browned. Add the garlic and the Swiss chard. Stir to combine, then add the veal shank, veal shank reduction and tomatoes.

Add the cavatappi noodles and toss to combine. Toss in the basil, butter and green onions. Sprinkle with blue cheese and serve in pasta bowls.

Ingredients

12 large		portobello mushrooms, peeled
$\frac{1}{4}$ cup	• 50 mL	olive oil
3 Tbsp.	• 45 mL	unsalted butter
2 cloves		garlic, minced
2 lbs.	• 1 kg	spinach, washed and stemmed
1 Tbsp.	• 15 mL	thyme, chopped
1 Tbsp.	• 15 mL	rosemary, chopped
$\frac{1}{4}$ cup	• 50 mL	grated aged cheddar cheese
1 cup	• 250 mL	Tomato Sauce (see page 229)

Oven-Roasted Portobello Mushrooms
with Red Wine Blue Cheese Sauce

I worked for a short time at The Inn at Little Washington, Virginia and was inspired by a dish they called "Portobello Mushrooms Pretending To Be Filet Mignon." This was actually a very clever idea because portobello mushrooms are very meaty and pair well with aged Cabernet Sauvignon. Also, the Cabernet Sauvignon can exhibit some mushroom characteristics as it ages. This recipe is dedicated to my happy memories of working at the Inn at Little Washington and is inspired by Chef Patrick O'Connell.

Preheat oven to 475°F (240°C).

Combine the portobello mushrooms with the olive oil in a large bowl and toss to combine thoroughly. Place the mushrooms on an ovenproof tray and bake for 15 minutes, or until they are golden brown.

Meanwhile, in a large sauté pan set over medium heat add the butter. When the butter is frothy add the garlic and sauté until it is golden brown. Sauté the spinach with the garlic until it has wilted, about 2 minutes. Toss the herbs with the spinach and remove the pan from the heat.

Divide the sautéed spinach among the portobello mushrooms then sprinkle the tops with the aged cheddar cheese. Make 6 stacks of 2 portobello mushrooms with spinach/cheese topping. Spoon over the tomato sauce and red wine blue cheese sauce (page 276).

MAKES 6 SERVINGS
recipe continued on next page

Ingredients

2 cups	•	500 mL	**Cabernet Sauvignon**
1			**shallot, finely minced**
1 tsp.	•	5 mL	**crushed black peppercorns**
1			**leek (white part only), finely minced**
1			**bay leaf**
2 Tbsp.	•	30 mL	**blue cheese**
1 Tbsp.	•	15 mL	**unsalted butter**
			kosher salt and white pepper to taste

Red Wine Blue Cheese Sauce

Pour the wine into a small saucepan and bring to a boil over high heat. Add the shallot, pepper, leek and bay leaf. Reduce the liquid until ½ cup (125 mL) remains. Strain the liquid into another small pot. Add the cheese and the butter and warm the sauce over low heat until they have melted. Blend the sauce with a whisk and season with salt and pepper.

Spring

Icewine Crème Brûlée Tart

Red Wine Ice Cream

White Chocolate Gewürztraminer
   Mousse and Lemon Parfait

Summer

Cherry Clafoutis

Peaches Caramelized
   with Clover Honey, Icewine
   and Fresh Basil

Summer Fruit Baked
   with Honey, Mint and Icewine

Icewine Savarin
   with Icewine Granite

Apricot Brioche
   with Icewine Edible Flower Sabayon

Desserts

Autumn

Pumpkin Cheesecake
  with Cranberry Compote

Tart Tatin

Cabernet Poached Pears Stuffed
  with Walnut and Mascarpone

Winter

Hillebrand Estate's Icewine Truffles

Chocolate Soufflé

Almond Chocolate Cake
  with Praline Meringue Parfait

Chocolate State of Mind

Ingredients

½ cup	•	125 mL	**unsalted butter**
1 cup	•	250 mL	**icing sugar**
5			**egg yolks**
1¾ cups	•	420 mL	**all-purpose flour (+ for dusting)**

Icewine Crème Brûlée Tart

Crème brûlée is the dessert darling of the past few years. It is on virtually every menu. My version incorporates icewine into the custard and, for extra texture, I bake it in a tart shell. It makes for a truly "wow" presentation and even better taste.

In the bowl of a stand mixer, with the machine set on medium, cream the butter and the icing sugar until fluffy and pale. Add the egg yolks one at a time and mix well to combine. Slowly add the flour and mix just to combine. Turn out the dough onto a lightly dusted surface and roll to a thickness of ½ inch (1 cm). The dough will be very delicate and soft so be gentle when rolling it out.

Line 6 lightly greased and floured 4-inch (10-cm) tart pans with dough and trim off the excess. Refrigerate for 30 minutes.

Preheat oven to 325°F (160°C).

Line the tart shells with parchment paper or aluminum foil and blind bake for 20 minutes or until light brown, then remove from the oven and let cool to room temperature.

MAKES 6 TARTS

recipe continued on next page

Ingredients

½ bottle ·	180 mL	**icewine**
1		**lemon, juice of**
½ cup ·	125 mL	**water**
4		**eggs, separated**
1 cup ·	250 mL	**granulated sugar**
1 Tbsp. ·	15 mL	**cornstarch**
3 Tbsp. ·	45 mL	**all-purpose flour**

for the brûlée filling

Combine the icewine, lemon juice and water in a small saucepan. Bring to a boil and turn off the heat.

Beat the egg yolks with the sugar, cornstarch and flour. Slowly pour about one-third of the wine mix into the yolks, whisking steadily. Pour the yolks back into the saucepan with the wine. Return to medium heat and cook, whisking constantly, until the mixture is thick and a few bubbles rise to the surface, about 10 minutes.

Using a rubber spatula, pour the custard into a clean bowl and cool for 5 minutes, stirring occasionally. Whisk the whites of the eggs until stiff, and slowly add to the cooked custard then combine well with a spatula. Pour the brûlée mixture into the tart shells.

Use a kitchen torch or a broiler set to high to caramelize the tops of the tarts. Serve immediately.

Ingredients

3 cups	• 750 mL	**red wine**
½ stick		**cinnamon**
2		**cloves**
1½ cups	• 375 mL	**unsalted butter, cubed**
1 cup	• 250 mL	**granulated sugar**
1		**vanilla pod, halved**
8		**egg yolks**

Red Wine Ice Cream

I believe you will enjoy this unusual ice cream. A few years ago, I experimented with making icicles based on wine. "Riesling-cicle," "Gewürzt-cicle," I thought the concept was good, but one thing led to another and this recipe was the end result. Not a "Wine-cicle," but rather a full-flavored ice cream.

Combine the red wine with the cinnamon and cloves in a saucepan set over medium heat. Bring to a boil then reduce the heat until the wine has reduced by half.

In the meantime, prepare a bowl full of ice cubes and reserve. Strain the reduced wine through a fine sieve into a stainless steel bowl to remove the cinnamon and clove.

Let the reduced wine cool to room temperature then combine with the butter, sugar, vanilla and egg yolks. Whisk to combine then set the bowl over simmering water and whisk vigorously for 15 minutes until the wine/egg mix looks smooth and soft. Remove the bowl from the heat and place on the ice bath to reduce the temperature quickly.

Pour the red wine custard into an ice cream machine and process as per the manufacturer's instructions.

Ingredients

3			**whole eggs**
1			**egg yolk**
$^3/_4$ cup	·	175 mL	**granulated sugar**
$^1/_2$ cup	·	125 mL	**fresh lemon juice**
2			**lemons, zest of, blanched and finely chopped**
$^1/_2$ cup	·	125 mL	**unsalted butter, cubed**
$^1/_4$ cup	·	50 mL	**35% cream, whipped**

White Chocolate Gewürztraminer
Mousse and Lemon Parfait

This recipe is about balance. The sweetness and distinct flavor of white chocolate playing opposite lemon not only tastes great but also makes for a beautiful presentation. Serve it in long tall glasses and top it off with some crunchy tuiles or biscotti.

Combine all the ingredients except the butter and cream in a stainless steel bowl and place the bowl over simmering water. Whisk continuously until the ingredients become pale and double in volume, about 20 minutes.

Remove the bowl from the heat and add the butter, a cube or two at a time, stirring constantly until the butter has blended into the lemon curd. Refrigerate the lemon curd for 1 hour, or until slightly chilled.

Fold in the whipped cream and gently combine until well mixed. Keep chilled.

to serve

Fill tall glasses with alternating layers of lemon parfait and Gewürztraminer mousse. Wait until each layer is set before adding the next. Garnish with biscotti or other cookies, if you wish.

Garnish with cabernet syrup (page 285), whipped cream and lemon balm or mint.

MAKES 6 SERVINGS

Ingredients

3 cups	·	750 mL	Gewürztraminer
1/3 cup	·	75 mL	granulated sugar
4			egg yolks
3 leaves			gelatin, soaked in cold water until soft
1/2 cup	·	125 mL	melted white chocolate
1/2 cup	·	125 mL	whipped 35% cream

for the Gewürztraminer mousse

Place the wine in a small saucepan and gently simmer until reduced by three-quarters.

In a stainless steel bowl combine the sugar, egg yolks and reduced wine. Set the bowl over simmering water and whisk until the ingredients become light and fluffy and doubled in volume. Take the gelatin leaves out of the water and squeeze out excess water.

Melt the gelatin in a small pot over low heat, about 5 minutes. Pour the gelatin into the mousse and mix quickly and thoroughly to combine.

Move the bowl off the heat and add the melted white chocolate. (Work quickly because the chocolate will set quickly.) Fold in the whipped cream.

Ingredients

| 2 cups | · | 500 mL | Cabernet Sauvignon |
| 1 cup | · | 250 mL | Simple Syrup (page 300) |

Cabernet Syrup

Combine ingredients in a small saucepan and place over low heat. Simmer until reduced by half. Remove from the heat and let cool to room temperature. Reserve, refrigerated, until required.

MAKES 1 1/2 CUPS (375 ML)

Ingredients

2 Tbsp. ·	30 mL	**softened unsalted butter**
2 Tbsp. ·	30 mL	**all-purpose flour**
4		**eggs**
6 Tbsp. ·	90 mL	**granulated sugar**
1		**vanilla bean, scraped and seeds removed**
½ tsp. ·	2.5 mL	**kosher salt**
1 Tbsp. ·	15 mL	**icewine**
1 cup ·	250 mL	**all-purpose flour**
1 cup ·	250 mL	**milk**
4 cups ·	1 L	**cherries, pitted**

Cherry Clafoutis

There is no better way to taste the full flavor of summer fruit than to prepare it in clafoutis. This is a recipe that evokes simple country charm and pleasures. The success of this recipe depends on the quality of the ingredients. Use only fresh ripe fruit in season.

Preheat oven to 350°F (180°C).

Butter and flour (using the 2 Tbsp./30mL flour) a 12-inch (3.5 L) ovenproof casserole.

Combine the eggs and sugar in the bowl of a stand mixer and, with the machine on high speed, beat until frothy and pale. Add the vanilla seeds, salt and icewine. Turn the the mixer to slow and whisk in the 1 cup (250 mL) of flour in a slow, steady stream followed by the milk.

Pour one-third of the batter into the prepared casserole. Distribute the cherries in a thin layer over the batter. Pour the remaining batter over the cherries and bake for 40 minutes or until the batter is set and is golden brown.

Remove from the oven and serve immediately.

MAKES 6 SERVINGS

Ingredients

¼ cup	50 mL	**unsalted butter**
6		**ripe peaches, halved and stones removed**
2 Tbsp.	30 mL	**clover honey**
1 Tbsp.	15 mL	**water**
2 Tbsp.	30 mL	**granulated sugar**
¼ cup	50 mL	**icewine**
2 Tbsp.	30 mL	**35% cream**
dash		**vanilla extract**
4		**basil leaves, thinly sliced**
3 cups	750 mL	**vanilla ice cream**

Peaches Caramelized
with Clover Honey, Icewine and Fresh Basil

Many pastry chefs are crossing over the savory threshhold to borrow herbs and spices to incorporate into creative and original desserts. When I worked at Langdon Hall Country House Hotel, my chef, Nigel Didcock, combined ripe peaches and basil in a dessert. It was a taste revelation to me and further proof that Chef Nigel was ahead of his time.

Preheat oven to 475°F (240°C).

In a large, heavy-bottomed ovenproof sauté pan set over medium heat, melt the butter. When the butter is frothy, add the peaches, cut-side down. Place the pan in the oven and roast the peaches for 15–20 minutes, or until the skins begin to wrinkle and pull away from the flesh.

Remove the peaches from the oven and, when cool enough to handle, peel then return the peaches to the pan.

Set the pan over medium-high heat and add the clover honey, water and sugar.

Allow the peaches to caramelize for 5 minutes then add the icewine and the cream. Bring the sauce to a boil, reduce the heat to a simmer and allow the sauce to thicken slightly, about 3 minutes.

Add the vanilla extract and the basil and stir to incorporate.

Carefully lift the peaches onto a platter or individual plates and serve with ice cream.

MAKES 6 SERVINGS

Ingredients

6 cups	· 1.5 L	**summer fruit, seeds, pits and stones removed**
½ cup	· 125 mL	**icewine**
1 Tbsp.	· 15 mL	**ginger, julienned**
¼ cup	· 50 mL	**unsalted butter, melted**
2 Tbsp.	· 30 mL	**bramble bush honey (or regular honey)**
1 tsp.	· 5 mL	**lemon thyme, finely chopped**
1 tsp.	· 5 mL	**mint, finely chopped**
1 tsp.	· 5 mL	**cinnamon, freshly grated**
pinch		**kosher salt**

Summer Fruit Baked
with Honey, Mint and Icewine

Cooking fruit in this manner is a reflection of my belief that I should not tamper with the raw materials Mother Nature has left for me to use. Use only the ripest and most beautiful seasonal fruit you can buy. Let your guests open the parcels as soon as they are pulled from the oven for maximum "wow" factor. This is particularly good with vanilla ice cream.

Preheat oven to 400°F (200°C).

Lay out 6 pieces of parchment paper, each piece approximately 12 inches (30 cm) square.

Combine all the ingredients in a large mixing bowl. Place equal amounts of the mixed fruit on each piece of parchment. Fold the parchment in half horizontally.

Pinch the edges of the paper together and crumple them to seal in the ingredients.

Place the parcels on a baking sheet and bake for 20 minutes.

Serve immediately and let the guests cut open their own parcel to release the aromas.

MAKES 6 SERVINGS

Ingredients

1 Tbsp.	·	15 mL	**dry yeast**
¹⁄₂ cup	·	125 mL	**warm milk**
3 cups	·	750 mL	**all-purpose flour**
¹⁄₂ cup	·	125 mL	**unsalted butter** (plus 2 Tbsp. · 30 mL)
3 Tbsp.	·	45 mL	**granulated sugar**
¹⁄₂ tsp.	·	15 mL	**kosher salt**
1			**lemon zest**
4			**eggs**

Icewine Savarin
with Icewine Granite

Icewine is one of the treasures found in the Niagara region. I believe that in the future icewine will be viewed on par with the other great treasures of the culinary world. Like foie gras, caviar and truffles, it has an aura. Icewine has been called "dessert in a glass" and I agree. "Savarin" is a French word meaning a dessert made from a yeast cake, rum and whipped cream.

Combine the yeast with the warm milk and stir to dissolve. Sift the flour into a bowl and make a well in the center. Add the yeast and the warm milk. Combine the mixture with a spatula.

In a small saucepan over medium heat melt the butter. Remove from the heat and let cool to room temperature. Add the sugar, salt, lemon zest and eggs. Whisk to combine but do not let it get airy or frothy.

Add the butter mix to the flour/yeast and work to incorporate thoroughly. Cover the bowl and allow to rest in a warm spot for 15 minutes.

Butter and flour a savarin ring (or doughnut ring) and fill it halfway with the savarin dough. Cover with a tea towel and let rise until doubled, about 20 minutes.

Preheat oven to 325°F (160°C).

Bake the savarin for 15 minutes or until set.

MAKES ONE 12-INCH (30-CM) SAVARIN RING

recipe continued on next page

Ingredients

1 cup	·	250 mL	**water**
1 cup	·	250 mL	**granulated sugar**
1 cup	·	250 mL	**icewine**
2 Tbsp.	·	30 mL	**apricot jam**
1 tsp.	·	5 mL	**cloves**
½ stick			**cinnamon**

for the icewine syrup

Mix all the ingredients together and bring to a boil over high heat. Reduce the heat and simmer for 20 minutes or until the syrup has thickened slightly.

Strain the syrup through a fine mesh sieve and let cool to room temperature. Set aside.

Ingredients

1 cup	·	250 mL	**icewine**
1			**lime, juice and zest of**
1			**lemon, juice and zest of**
½ cup	·	125 mL	**water**
½ cup	·	125 mL	**granulated sugar**

Icewine Granite

Mix the ingredients together in a saucepan and bring to a boil. Remove from the heat and let stand for 10 minutes. Strain the liquid through a fine mesh sieve into a bowl and freeze.

Every 15 minutes return to the freezer and scrape the granite with a fork to make it "slushy" looking.

To serve, scrape off the top of the granite with an ice cream scoop and serve.

Ingredients

¼ cup	• 50 mL	**warm milk**
2 tsp.	• 10 mL	**fresh yeast**
⅔ cup	• 150 mL	**all-purpose flour** (plus 3 Tbsp. • 45 mL)
1½ cups	• 375 mL	**bread flour** (plus 3 Tbsp. • 45 mL)
2 Tbsp.	• 30 mL	**granulated sugar** (plus .5 tsp. • 2.5 mL)
1 tsp.	• 5 mL	**kosher salt**
3		**eggs**
½ cup	• 125 mL	**unsalted butter, cubed, at room temperature**

Apricot Brioche
with Icewine Edible Flower Sabayon

In this recipe I layer butter-sautéed brioche between poached apricots and edible flower sabayon. By glazing the sabayon first we intensify its flavor and make a dramatic presentation. This recipe would make a welcome addition to any brunch dessert table.

Pour the milk over the yeast in a small bowl and let sit for several minutes. Stir to dissolve the yeast. Combine the flours, sugar and salt in a large mixing bowl. Add the milk and eggs and mix on low speed in a stand mixer, fitted with a dough hook, until the dough pulls together.

Add the butter a cube at a time and continue to mix for 3–5 minutes, scraping occasionally or until the dough is smooth and pulls away from the sides of the bowl. The dough will seem very soft and glossy.

Place the dough in loaf pans, cover with plastic wrap and set in a warm place to rise for 1 hour, or until dough doubles in volume.

Bake at 375°F (190°C), for 35 to 40 minutes or until golden brown.

When ready, remove from the loaf pans and let cool on a wire rack.

MAKES 6 SERVINGS

recipe continued on next page

1 cup	·	250 mL	**water**
1 cup	·	250 mL	**granulated sugar**
24			**ripe apricots, halved and stones discarded**

for the poached apricots

Combine the water and sugar and bring to a boil. Reduce the heat to a simmer and add the apricots. Simmer the apricots for 10 minutes, or until they become soft, but are not falling apart. Remove from the heat and let cool to room temperature.

Pour out $\frac{1}{2}$ cup (50 mL) of syrup and reserve. Keep the apricots in the remaining syrup.

Ingredients

6			**egg yolks**
$\frac{1}{4}$ cup	·	50 mL	**Simple Syrup (page 300)**
2 Tbsp.	·	30 mL	**icewine**
$\frac{1}{4}$ cup	·	50 mL	**35% cream, whipped**
$\frac{1}{2}$ cup	·	125 mL	**edible flower petals**

Icewine Edible Flower Sabayon

Combine the egg yolks with the simple syrup in a double boiler, or a stainless steel bowl fitted over a pot of simmering water, and whisk continuously for 15 minutes, or until thick. Add the icewine and stir to combine. Add the whipped cream and the edible flowers. Reserve.

to serve

| 2 Tbsp. | · | 30 mL | **unsalted butter** |

Slice the brioche. Melt the butter in a large sauté pan and sauté the brioche until golden brown, about 3 minutes per side. On 6 large plates make alternating layers of sautéed brioche, poached apricots and edible flower sabayon.

Ingredients

3 cups	• 750 mL	**cream cheese**
3		**eggs**
1 cup	• 250 mL	**granulated sugar**
1 tsp.	• 5 mL	**vanilla**
½ tsp.	• 2.5 mL	**ground ginger**
2 tsp.	• 10 mL	**ground cinnamon**
1 cup	• 250 mL	**good quality canned pumpkin purée**

Pumpkin Cheesecake
with Cranberry Compote

This book would not be complete if this pumpkin cheesecake recipe were not included. For some reason, it's the only cheesecake I like, perhaps because it is so festive; the taste of pumpkin always creates a feeling of holiday cheer. I like to prepare this for our family Thanksgiving dinner and it is always a big hit.

Preheat oven to 300˚F (150˚C).

In a stand mixer on high speed, cream the cream cheese with the eggs until light and fluffy. Add the sugar to the cheese mixture and beat for 7 minutes. Stir in the spices and fold in the pumpkin purée.

Pour batter into an 8-inch (20-cm) springform pan.

Bake for 40 minutes or until set. Allow cheesecake to cool in the oven with the door slightly opened.

MAKES 1 TART

Ingredients

1 cup	• 250 mL	**cranberries**
1		**lemon, zest and juice of**
½ cup	• 125 mL	**granulated sugar**
½		**cinnamon stick**
½ cup	• 125 mL	**water**
3 Tbsp.	• 45 mL	**dried cherries**
2		**oranges, juice and zest of**
1		**clove**

Cranberry Compote

Combine all the ingredients in a saucepan set over medium heat and bring to a boil. Reduce heat and simmer, stirring frequently.

When the compote has thickened, about 15 minutes, remove from the heat and let cool to room temperature. Remove the cinnamon stick.

Serve with cheesecake.

Tart Tatin

Tart tatin is a classic French dessert that can be made with many fruits, including apricots, plums, pears and apples. I have included this classic recipe as a small token of respect for the many great chefs who have forged a profession that is respected and esteemed the world over. To those chefs, both acclaimed and unsung, thank you for making it possible for me to succeed on my own terms.

Ingredients

1 lb.	•	500 g	**apples**
¼ cup	•	50 mL	**unsalted butter**
¼ cup	•	50 mL	**granulated sugar**

Peel, halve and core the apples.

Melt the butter in a heavy-bottomed ovenproof pan and sprinkle in the sugar. Arrange the apple halves in the sugar and butter mix with the cored side up. Cover the pan tightly. Cook the apples until they begin to caramelize, 15–20 minutes.

Remove from the heat and let the apples cool slightly in the pan.

MAKES 1 TART

recipe continued on next page

Ingredients

1½ lbs. •	750 g	**all-purpose flour**
7 Tbsp. •	105 mL	**cold butter, cubed**
2		**egg yolks**
½ tsp. •	2.5 mL	**kosher salt**
2 tsp. •	10 mL	**granulated sugar**
3 Tbsp. •	45 mL	**water**
1		**egg, slightly beaten**

for the pâté brisée

Preheat oven to 350°F (180°C).

Pour the flour onto a clean work surface and make a well in the center. Add the butter, egg yolks, salt, sugar and water. Working with your fingertips, mix the ingredients and gradually draw the flour into the center until it resembles coarse crumbs. Gather the dough and knead it just until it comes together in a ball. Chill for 1 hour.

Roll out the dough to a circle roughly the size of the pan used to cook the apples and about ¼ inch (5 mm) thick.

Cover the apples with the circle of dough and brush with the egg. Bake until golden brown, about 20 minutes. Remove the pan from the heat and let cool for 5 minutes. Carefully invert the tart onto a plate. Let cool to room temperature then slice and serve.

Ingredients

3 cups	•	750 mL	**Cabernet Sauvignon**
1 cup	•	250 mL	**Simple Syrup**
1 stick			**cinnamon**
2 tsp.	•	10 mL	**vanilla extract**
1			**lemon, juice of**
8			**ripe pears**

Cabernet Poached Pears
Stuffed with Walnut and Mascarpone

Poached pears are synonymous with wine country. This versatile recipe can be dressed up or down to suit the occasion, but it will always be very tasty. The pears are poached in Cabernet Sauvignon then stuffed and roasted in the oven for a light caramelization.

Combine the ingredients in a saucepan large enough to hold the 8 pears. Place the pan over medium-high heat. Bring it to a boil, then reduce the heat and simmer, just until the pears are cooked through, about 20 minutes. Remove the pan from the heat and let the pears cool to room temperature in the poaching liquid.

When the pears are cool enough to handle, carefully lift them out of the poaching liquid and use a small spoon to scoop out the core from the bottom of the pear. Reserve 6 pears in the refrigerator until required. Chop the remaining 2 pears into small dice and reserve for the pear filling.

MAKES 6 SERVINGS

Ingredients

1 cup	•	250 mL	**water**
1 cup	•	250 mL	**granulated sugar**

Simple Syrup

Combine the ingredients in a small saucepan and place over medium heat. Simmer for 5 minutes then remove from the heat and let cool to room temperature. Reserve, refrigerated, until required.

MAKES 2 CUPS (500 ML)

Ingredients

$\frac{1}{2}$ cup	· 125 mL	**mascarpone cheese, at room temperature**
2		**egg yolks**
2 Tbsp.	· 30 mL	**pear poaching liquid**
2		**poached pears, diced**
$\frac{1}{4}$ cup	· 50 mL	**lightly toasted walnuts, chopped**
6		**mint leaves, chopped**

for the pear filling

In the bowl of a stand mixer, combine all the ingredients well. Do not overmix the filling. Transfer the filling to another bowl and refrigerate for 1 hour until set.

Using a small spoon, scoop out the filling and press it into the bottom of the reserved pears. Use all of the filling and once all 6 pears are stuffed return them to the refrigerator.

Ingredients

$\frac{1}{4}$ cup	· 50 mL	**unsalted butter**
2 Tbsp.	· 30 mL	**honey**
pinch		**kosher salt**

to roast the stuffed pears

Preheat oven to 350°F (180°C).

In a large sauté pan set over medium heat, melt the butter and the honey. Add the stuffed pears to the pan and gently shake the pan so the pears roll around in the butter and honey. Season the stuffed pears with a pinch of salt and transfer to the oven. Roast the pears, turning them every so often, until they are golden brown, about 10 minutes. Remove from the oven and serve.

Ingredients

1 lb.	•	500 g	**chocolate, chopped into small pieces**
1¼ cups	•	300 mL	**35% cream**
½			**vanilla bean**
¼ cup	•	50 mL	**icewine**
2 Tbsp.	•	30 mL	**unsalted butter**

Hillebrand Estate's Icewine Truffles

Here is one of our most sought-after recipes.

Place the chopped chocolate in a stainless steel bowl.

Add the cream, vanilla and half the icewine to a small saucepan set over medium heat. Bring to a boil and remove the vanilla bean.

Using a small knife, scrape out the seeds from the vanilla bean and return them to the cream. Discard the bean.

Pour the hot cream over the chopped chocolate and stir gently until the chocolate has melted completely. Add the butter in small pieces. When the butter has melted and incorporated into the chocolate/cream mixture, transfer the truffle base into a flat casserole, using a rubber spatula to get every drop.

Refrigerate the chocolate truffle base until it is set, about 2 hours. Remove the chocolate truffle base and, using a small teaspoon, form 1-oz. (30-g) balls. Repeat until all chocolate has been formed into balls.

Refrigerate the truffles until all the chocolate has been used. Dust the truffles with cocoa powder or icing sugar and serve.

MAKE 3–4 DOZEN

Ingredients

3 Tbsp.	•	45 mL	**softened unsalted butter**
2 Tbsp.	•	30 mL	**granulated sugar**
3 oz.	•	90 g	**chopped chocolate**
1/4 cup	•	50 mL	**cocoa powder**
1 cup	•	250 mL	**milk**
1			**vanilla bean, split**
1/4 cup	•	50 mL	**unsalted butter**
1/2 cup	•	125 mL	**all-purpose flour**
5			**egg whites**
4			**egg yolks**
6 Tbsp.	•	90 mL	**granulated sugar**

Chocolate Soufflé

Preparing soufflé at home can be a pleasurable experience and can make your reputation as a home chef. Follow these instructions carefully for a result that is at once light, airy, tall and intensely flavored.

Rub the insides of 8 ramekins (4 oz./125 g each) with the softened butter. Divide the 2 Tbsp. (30 mL) of sugar among the ramekins and shake each ramekin to coat the insides with a thin layer of sugar. Pour out any excess sugar and discard.

In a small saucepan set over low heat bring the chocolate, cocoa powder, milk and vanilla bean to a boil. Take out the vanilla bean and scrape any seeds that remain in the bean back into the milk. Make a paste with the butter and the flour. Add the boiling chocolate milk, a little at a time, until it has bound the chocolate and made it thick. Stir constantly to form a smooth base, about 5 minutes.

Remove the saucepan from the heat and stir one egg white into the still-hot chocolate base. Using a whisk, beat the mixture until smooth, making sure that no lumps appear. Transfer the chocolate base to a bowl and add one egg yolk at a time, stirring after each addition to incorporate thoroughly.

Preheat oven to 350°F (180°C).

Combine the remaining egg whites with the 6 Tbsp. (90 mL) of sugar in a stand mixer and process on high speed until the egg whites have formed stiff peaks. Stir the egg whites into the chocolate/egg base in 3 additions. Make sure after each addition that the stiff egg whites are incorporated gently and thoroughly.

Pour the chocolate soufflé mixture into the prepared ramekins to half full. Place in a bain-marie in the oven and bake for 30 minutes. Serve immediately.

MAKES 8 SERVINGS

Ingredients

$\frac{1}{2}$ lb.	•	250 g	**bitter chocolate**
1 cup	•	250 mL	**unsalted butter**
$1\frac{1}{2}$ cups	•	375 mL	**icing sugar**
$\frac{1}{3}$ cup	•	75 mL	**brown sugar**
6			**eggs, separated**
$\frac{3}{4}$ cup	•	175 mL	**ground almonds**
$\frac{1}{3}$ cup	•	75 mL	**all-purpose flour**

Almond Chocolate Cake
with Praline Meringue Parfait

I love chocolate cake. I love it warm, room temperature, cold or frozen. I also love praline. It seemed logical for me to combine two of my favorite sweets to create something different, but also delicious.

Preheat oven to 325°F (160°C). Grease eight 4-inch (10-cm) springform pans and reserve.

Melt the chocolate in a stainless steel bowl over simmering water. Combine the butter and the two sugars in the bowl of a stand mixer and beat at medium speed until pale and thick. Add the egg yolks one at a time until well incorporated. Add the melted chocolate and mix. Add the almonds and flour and mix to combine thoroughly. Whip 4 egg whites to stiff peaks. (Reserve the remaining whites for another use.) Fold into the chocolate batter and mix carefully to combine.

Pour the batter into the prepared pans and bake for 35 minutes, or until a toothpick inserted in the middle of the cake comes out clean. Let the cakes cool to room temperature then remove them from the pans.

MAKES 8 SERVINGS

recipe continued on next two pages

Ingredients

$^{3}/_{4}$ cup	·	175 mL	**granulated sugar**
$^{3}/_{4}$ cup	·	175 mL	**slivered almonds**

for the praline dust

Prepare a cookie sheet with a lightly greased piece of aluminum foil or parchment paper and reserve.

Pour the sugar into a small heavy-bottomed pan and place over low heat. Gently heat the sugar until it begins to melt, about 8 minutes. Increase the heat to medium and cook the sugar until it turns a brilliant golden caramel color then quickly fold in the slivered almonds and stir to combine. Turn out the praline onto the prepared cookie sheet. Use a spatula to flatten the praline, and let cool to room temperature.

When the praline is cool to the touch and brittle, break it into pieces and place the pieces in a food processor. Pulse until the praline is the texture of granulated sugar.

Ingredients

4			**egg whites**
$^{1}/_{2}$ cup	·	125 mL	**granulated sugar**
$^{3}/_{4}$ cup	·	175 mL	**35% cream**
1 cup	·	250 mL	**praline dust**

for the meringue parfait

Using a stand mixer set on high speed, whisk the egg whites to soft peaks. Add the sugar and continue whisking until firm peaks form. In a separate bowl, whip the cream to firm peaks. Fold the whipped cream into the whipped meringue.

Add the praline dust and mix to combine. Pour the praline meringue into a container and place in the freezer until just set.

Ingredients

1 Tbsp. ·	15 mL	**unsalted butter**
1 Tbsp. ·	15 mL	**granulated sugar**
4		**ripe pears, peeled, cored and quartered**
2 tsp. ·	10 mL	**honey**
1 Tbsp. ·	15 mL	**icewine**

for the honey roasted pears

Preheat oven to 325°F (160°C).

In a large sauté pan set over medium heat, combine the butter and sugar. When the mixture begins to bubble, add the pears, honey and icewine. Transfer the pan to the oven and cook for 15 minutes, or until golden brown.

To serve, place slices of the chocolate cake on 8 serving plates and top each slice with a scoop of the praline meringue parfait. Serve with honey roasted pears.

Ingredients

³/₄ cup	•	175 mL	**egg yolks**
¹/₃ cup	•	75 mL	**granulated sugar**
1 cup	•	250 mL	**good-quality bitter chocolate, melted**
2 cups	•	500 mL	**unsalted butter, softened**
1 ¹/₃ cups	•	325 mL	**Dutch process cocoa powder**
1 ¹/₄ cups	•	300 mL	**35% cream**
³/₄ cup	•	75 mL	**35% cream, whipped**
¹/₃ cup	•	75 mL	**granulated sugar**

Chocolate State of Mind

Chocolate lovers will understand my need to include a dessert so intensely chocolate it will cause your eyes to roll. This is the Chocolate State of Mind. This is the real deal. Serve it in as natural a state as possible; any garnish or sauce will only dilute the experience. This recipe can be kept in the freezer, tightly wrapped in plastic, for 3 months. Let it thaw in the refrigerator overnight before serving.

Combine the eggs and ¹/₃ cup (75 mL) of the sugar in the bowl of a stand mixer set on high speed until the mixture is pale and has thickened to approximately twice its original volume.

Turn the speed of the mixer to low, add the melted chocolate in a steady stream and mix until fully blended.

In a separate bowl, combine the softened butter and the cocoa powder and, with a rubber spatula, work it to form a paste. With the speed of the mixer set to medium speed, add the butter/cocoa paste to the chocolate/egg mixture and mix to combine. The mixture may look coarse or curdled but keep mixing until it becomes a smooth paste, about 15 minutes.

Lower the speed of the mixer to low and pour in the 1 ¹/₄ cups (300 mL) of cream. When well combined, stop the mixer and, using a rubber spatula, scrape out the chocolate mixture into a clean bowl.

In a separate bowl, add the whipped cream to the ¹/₃ cup (75 mL) sugar and fold this into the chocolate mix. Stir to combine well.

Pour this mix into a 12-inch (30-cm) terrine mold and refrigerate until set. To serve, remove the chocolate terrine from the refrigerator and unmold onto a clean cutting surface. Slice the terrine and serve.

MAKES ONE 12-INCH (30-CM) TERRINE